BATLA HOUSE

Karnal Singh, a 1984-batch IPS officer and an engineer from the Delhi College of Engineering (DCE) and the Indian Institute of Technology (IIT) Kanpur, has over 34 years of experience in the investigation of corruption, terrorism, money laundering and criminal cases. In Delhi Police Special Cell, he spearheaded the investigation of the 2008 Delhi blast cases, which led to the Batla House encounter. He is a recipient of President's Police Medal for Distinguished Service and Police Medal for Meritorious Service.

BATLA HOUSE

AN ENCOUNTER THAT SHOOK THE NATION

KARNAL SINGH

RUPA

Published by
Rupa Publications India Pvt. Ltd 2020
7/16, Ansari Road, Daryaganj New Delhi 110002

Sales Centres:
Allahabad Bengaluru Chennai
Hyderabad Jaipur Kathmandu
Kolkata Mumbai

ISBN: 978-93-90260-37-9

Seventh impression 2022

10 9 8 7

Printed at Repro India Limited, India

In honour of
Mohan Chand Sharma
and the countless unsung heroes who have lost their lives
fighting against terrorism

CONTENTS

CONTENTS

PROLOGUE

19 September 2008

I was at the Delhi Police Special Cell office in Lodhi Colony. I looked at my watch. It was 10.45 a.m. Two teams were on their way to Batla House. Delhi had witnessed a devastating terrorist attack six days ago, on 13 September, by a terror outfit called the Indian Mujahideen (IM). The explosions in heavily crowded public places had claimed 22 lives and injured 131 people.

Special Cell teams had been working night and day since then to gather intelligence and trace the perpetrators. Our investigation and surveillance leads had raised suspicion on a particular resident of Flat no. 108, L-18, Batla House. We led our teams there that day to search and investigate further.

At around 11.00 a.m., my phone rang. It was a call from Inspector Mohan Chand Sharma, who was leading the first team. 'Sir, we are going in,' he said.

'All the best!' I replied and kept the phone down.

The next few minutes dragged on as I anxiously waited to know if we had found the suspected terrorists. Meanwhile, shots being fired were heard in the Batla House area.

Around 10 minutes after Mohan's call, my phone rang again. Assistant Commissioner of Police (ACP) Sanjeev Kumar Yadav was on the line. He spoke in a tearful voice. 'Sir, Mohan and Head Constable (HC) Balwant Singh have been shot and have sustained bullet injuries.'

I was shocked. 'What happened? Where are they?' I asked.

Sanjeev replied that they were being shifted to the hospital. He mentioned that terrorists were also injured and were inside the house.

I replied on the call, 'Sanjeev, we have to catch them alive... they are the key... I am on my way. I am also requisitioning additional force.'

'Yes, sir,' Sanjeev said.

More shots were heard in Batla House.

1

EYE FOR AN EYE: THE DUST WILL NEVER SETTLE DOWN

13 September 2008
(Six days before the Batla House shoot-out)

It was a quiet Saturday at home. I was engrossed in reading a book on science fiction. The television was playing in the background.

'*Chai chahiye?* (Do you want some tea?)' my wife, Renuka, asked me. I replied with a distracted 'hmm'. She went into the kitchen and I resumed reading.

A few minutes later, she came back with tea. My son, Archit, who was 13 years old at that time, came running to me with a notebook and a pencil in his hand. 'Papa, can you help me with this math problem?' he said, pointing to his notebook. I kept my book aside and started questioning him on the basics of math to gauge how much he already understood and the areas where he needed my help. I didn't get to spend enough time with my family on weekdays, so I cherished whatever little time I got with them over the weekends. My daughters, Shruti and Kritika, were already in college and we spoke more over the phone than in person. I patted my son's head as he sat on the floor and attempted to solve the problems.

Just then, my phone started ringing. *Who can it be on a Saturday evening?* I wondered. I picked up my phone to see the name of a journalist flashing on the screen.

'Hi, Vishal (name changed),' I answered the call.

'Sir, has there been a blast in Karol Bagh?'

Just then, my landline started ringing too. I was also getting another call on my mobile. It was from the Police Control Room (PCR).

'Let me call you back, Vishal. I have a call waiting.' I disconnected the call, fearing the worst.

I took the call from the PCR. There was indeed an explosion in Karol Bagh a few minutes ago. I told the PCR that I was leaving for the blast site. 'Have the Special Cell teams been informed?'

'Yes, sir, we are alerting all senior officers and field units as per protocol.'

My wife was getting a bit anxious. '*Kya hua? Sab theek hai?* (What happened? Is everything okay?)'

'There is a report of a bomb explosion in Karol Bagh. I am going there now,' I replied.

I called out to the driver to get ready to leave. I quickly put on a shirt as I answered a barrage of calls.

'Is anyone hurt?' my wife asked me, worried.

'I don't know yet. I will speak to you later,' I replied as I got into the car.

'Oh, where is Shruti?' I asked. Shruti, our eldest daughter, was in the third year of fashion designing at the National Institute of Fashion Technology (NIFT), Delhi.

'She is working on some project with her friends. After that, they will go to Lajpat Nagar or Nehru Place, I am not exactly sure, to buy some fabric,' my wife replied.

'Call and check on her, and ask her to come home immediately.'

'Okay, be safe,' my wife added and waved me goodbye.

On my way, I spoke to Shri Yudhvir Singh Dadwal, commissioner of police (CP), over the phone, to discuss the course of action. He told me that he had already declared a Red Alert[1] in the whole of Delhi.

I passed on the message to the police stations through the PCR instructing them to immediately deploy manpower in the hospitals where the injured were being taken. The police was asked to look for any vehicle that was left unattended in the vicinity of the hospitals.[2] I coordinated with the Special Cell officers to discuss which team members were to be engaged and assign tasks to them accordingly.

I had joined as the head of the Delhi Police Special Cell first as Additional Commissioner in January 2004 and continued after my promotion as Joint CP in June 2004. In recent years, the Special Cell had cracked many important cases of terrorism including the bomb explosions in Liberty and Satyam Cinema, and the Diwali blasts of 2005. The department is credited with arresting more than 200 dreaded gangsters and 140 terrorists, neutralizing 20 terrorists from various terror modules, preventing several attacks and neutralizing 56 criminals during my stint in the Special Cell.

The Special Cell of the Delhi Police is the specialized

---

[1]When Red Alert is declared, the entire police workforce is activated for strategic response. The PCR notifies all the police stations, border checkposts, traffic units and PCR vans to deploy maximum manpower on roads to conduct strategic checking throughout the city/state, and to all the senior officers to make proactive checks within their jurisdictions.

[2]During the Gujarat blasts of 2008, vehicles with bombs planted in them were parked near the hospitals to inflict more casualties on the visiting relatives of the injured and the dead. Hospitals are also important places to check after such incidents to ensure that in case the perpetrator/s is hurt during the explosion, he or she does not escape.

unit that deals specifically with counterterrorism. Its origin is linked to the growth of terrorism in India. The late 1970s saw the growth of terrorism in Punjab, and the late 1980s saw the beginning of jihadi terrorism in Jammu and Kashmir (J&K), which later spread to other parts of the country. Before the Special Cell was constituted, the Crime Branch of the Delhi Police was investigating terror-related cases besides investigating other serious criminal offences.

New Delhi houses Parliament, the Rashtrapati Bhavan (the president's official address), the prime minister's (PM) residence and office, foreign embassies, vital installations and iconic places. A number of VIPs also stay in Delhi. Any successful attempt by terrorists in Delhi gives them international media publicity. It was of utmost importance to have better intelligence collection on terror to prevent any such attack in the capital. Therefore, there was the need to have an agency that could specifically deal with the prevention and investigation of terrorist activities in Delhi. Keeping this in mind, the Ministry of Home Affairs vide its order dated 12 September 1988 formed a special unit (to be called Special Cell) in Delhi Police. The Special Cell had three field units: one located in Lodhi Colony, the second in Rohini and the third in New Friends Colony.

The officers posted in the Special Cell are handpicked and completely devoted to their missions, often working round the clock. They are driven solely by the aim of developing counterterror intelligence and cracking terror cases. There is no concept of weekends or holidays or working hours. They take a break only after the assigned case is solved. Till then, they live, breathe and work on the cases they are assigned to. Even the sun completes its day's journey at dusk, but the journey of a Special Cell officer is never ending; it continues incessantly from one case to another.

On the day of the blast, the Special Cell officers were listening into interceptions and planning strategic intelligence collection for several ongoing cases. One of the most important missions being planned at that time was in J&K. Inspector Mohan Chand Sharma, a veteran in anti-terror operations, was having a discussion with Sub-inspector (SI) Rahul Kumar Singh about the intelligence input received by the Special Cell team deployed at Pathankot, Punjab.

Mohan had been working in the Special Cell since 1998. He was an extremely brave and intelligent officer who was part of numerous operations. He had neutralized 35 terrorists and 40 gangsters during his tenure of 10 years. He had arrested 80 terrorists and more than a hundred dreaded criminals. He was a recipient of the President's Police Medal for Gallantry (PPMG) and had also received six police medals for gallantry. He also had an out-of-turn promotion to his credit.[3] He had a quiet and serious demeanour and was respected by his team members.

Rahul, a diligent and technology-savvy officer of the 1994 batch,[4] was posted in the Special Cell in 2002 and was generally assigned the investigation of important cases, as he was skilled at conducting field operations. He had received two gallantry medals and one out-of-turn promotion for his outstanding performance.

I had deployed a team of officers in J&K to intercept terror-related calls so that they could act against the terrorists based on these interceptions. The deployment had helped the Special Cell in nabbing and neutralizing many Kashmir-based terrorists

---

[3]The Delhi Police grants out-of-turn promotion (OTP) in rare cases of gallantry or for solving a very challenging case.
[4]For all inspectors and ACP, except Sanjeev Yadav, 'the batch' means batch of SIs. Sanjeev is from Delhi, Andaman and Nicobar Islands Police Service (DANIPS).

before they could strike. However, this move of the Special Cell became a bone of contention between the Delhi Police and the Government of J&K. The Government of J&K made a complaint to the Home Ministry, demanding to move the Delhi Police team out of J&K. Following this, the team was shifted from J&K to Pathankot. This Special Cell team had got the interception relating to some movements of terrorists in J&K. Mohan asked Inspector Sanjay Dutt to immediately move to Pathankot along with a team. They were planning for their trip to J&K when the office received information of the blast in Karol Bagh. Mohan immediately activated the Special Cell control room to deploy officers and teams.

Sanjay, a brave and intelligent officer, had worked on several terrorist cases in the Special Cell for the last 10 years. He had acquired a vast knowledge of J&K-based terrorist groups and terrorist organizations of North-eastern states, particularly Manipur. He had received two police medals for gallantry and also an out-of-turn promotion.

I had not even reached Karol Bagh when I received another call from the PCR informing me of another blast in Connaught Place (more commonly known as CP), another heavily crowded and one of the most popular marketplaces in Delhi. *How many more could be there and which other areas could be targeted?* I tried to think of the other places that were easy targets. Usually, terrorists target crowded places such as markets or religious places in order to inflict maximum damage to life and inculcate fear in people's minds.

Following the explosion at Connaught Place, the police was instructed to check dustbins throughout Delhi as the bomb there was planted in a dustbin. The wireless cracked with information on three more blasts by 6.35 p.m., taking the total count to five. Two bombs had exploded at Greater Kailash,

M-Block Market, one at Central Park, one at Barakhamba Road in Connaught Place and one at Karol Bagh. I had also instructed Ravi Shankar, assistant commissioner of police (ACP) of Special Cell and Sanjeev Kumar Yadav, ACP (Special Cell), to rush to the blast sites with their teams.

Ravi, a 1982-batch officer of the Delhi Police, had solved many cases of terrorism and international criminal gangs, and had arrested more than a hundred terrorists of different outfits. He had three work stints with me: one in the North-West District, second in the Crime Branch, where he was instrumental in working out the 42 blast cases of 1996–98 and third in the Special Cell. He was heading the Rohini office of the Special Cell at the time. He got two out-of-turn promotions—one from being SI to Inspector in 1989 and the second from Inspector to ACP in 1995 for his outstanding performance. He had received the PPMG, President's Police Medal for Distinguish Service and President's Police Medal for Meritorious Service.

Sanjeev, an officer with a commendable track record, had been handpicked by me to head the Lodhi Colony unit of the Special Cell. He joined the Special Cell in 2004. He had taken part in dozens of shoot-outs with hardcore inter-state criminals and terrorists in Delhi and other states including J&K. He had been awarded two gallantry medals.

I made a mental note of the other officers from the Special Cell who were needed on this case as their experience would be invaluable. I called Alok Kumar, deputy commissioner of police (DCP), Special Cell. Alok was on a leave to visit Vaishno Devi with his family. 'Alok, come back immediately, there have been several blasts in Delhi.'

Alok had a stellar service record. He had two work stints with me, one in the Crime Branch and second in the

Special Cell. He had handled more than a hundred successful operations in which notorious and dreaded gangsters as well as terrorists were arrested. He is a recipient of the PPMG, President's Police Medal for Meritorious Services and UN Medal for service with the United Nations Mission in Bosnia.

Karol Bagh

At 5.55 p.m., a powerful explosion had rocked the busy Karol Bagh market in North Delhi. Many calls had started pouring into the PCR and within minutes, the entire police force was activated for response. People who had called the PCR number (100), described hearing a deafening sound and seeing an autorickshaw being thrown up several feet above the ground. In the background, there were cries of injured people too.

On weekends, Delhi markets are usually bustling with energy as people come out to enjoy some time with their family and friends over shopping and street food. The roads are busy with honking cars, two-wheelers and three-wheelers jostling for a spot to park their vehicles. One can hear an excited chatter all around.

However, that day when I got off the car, there was an eerie silence. People who were enjoying with their loved ones moments ago, were now frightened and struck with distress.

By the time I reached the blast site, it had been cordoned off by the police. The injured had been shifted to hospitals by the local police and local people with the help of the PCR. As I walked towards the blast area, I saw several people standing with anxious and sad looks on their faces. They were looking for answers, whispering amongst each other in low voices. Many people from the press were standing outside the cordoned-off area. I walked in with Special Cell officers and local police to inspect the blast area. An autorickshaw was shredded to pieces. Some pieces of the yellow-and-black coloured metal were hanging from a tree. Many parts of the autorickshaw were found at a distance of 10–20 meters from the blast site. The CNG cylinder of the auto was found 10 meters away from the remains of the autorickshaw. Another autorickshaw, in a totally damaged condition, was found near the divider of the road. I asked Sanjeev to find out if the auto drivers had survived and if there were any eyewitnesses who could help with the investigation.

The road was strewn with damaged goods and parts of vehicles. I looked up and saw the windowpanes that had shattered due to the blast's impact. Blood was splattered on the road. I prayed to the Almighty, hoping those who were injured would soon recover from this.

My mind was filled with sadness. I had visited many a blast sites and each time I got very emotional seeing such loss of innocent lives and abject suffering. *Why do men kill men? What divine purpose could it serve?*

I took a closer look at the blast site and observed that the iron sheets of the autorickshaw had rough edges and not sharp ones. With my past experience of working on many blast sites, I knew that high explosives such as RDX resulted in sharp cuts, while low explosives (ammonium nitrate, potassium chlorate—almost all oxidizing agents act as explosives) resulted in blunt cuts. The smell of ammonium nitrate hung in the air, especially near the autorickshaw. I wanted to check with the forensic team to confirm my observation. However, it was already collecting evidences from the site and I knew that it would take some time for them to arrive at a conclusion.

I was informed that the CP was trying to reach me on my phone. Mobile phone services were jammed and wireless connections were the only way to communicate. He asked me to come to Central Park in Connaught Place at the earliest.

I asked Sanjeev to come with me and asked the rest of the team to complete the analysis of the blast site and meet us directly at the office.

Greater Kailash, M-Block Market

Meanwhile, Rahul and SI Dharmender Kumar reached the M-Block Market in Greater Kailash, where two successive explosions had taken place at 6.30 p.m. and 6.35 p.m.

Dharmender, a daring officer and an expert in undercover and covert operations, had been working in the Special Cell since 2003 and was an asset to the department. He had received one gallantry medal.

The first explosion took place in a dustbin opposite Shop no. M-9 (a Levi's store) and the second was opposite Shop no. M-29 (the popular Prince Paan shop). The injured were moved to nearby hospitals. Vehicles and shops were damaged. The bombs were planted in dustbins that had some holes and small cycle ball bearings. The officers assessed that the terrorists had planned the first bomb to explode at the Levi's store, which was in the middle of the market. Then as people would try to rush out of the market through the exit near Prince Paan Corner, the second bomb would explode causing maximum damage. They examined the blast sites further and looked for eyewitnesses and CCTV cameras that could help piece the investigation together.

Connaught Place

The police had searched all the dustbins, unattended items and parked vehicles to ensure that there were no more bombs planted. Timely action by the workforce had helped in detecting and defusing three live bombs planted in dustbins at Regal

Cinema, the children's park at India Gate and Central Park. Commissioner of Police, Shri Dadwal, had reached Central Park in Connaught Place. He along with other senior officers, inspected the blast site. The media was waiting outside the cordoned-off area to speak to him and the other officers. He discussed with me what information we could share with the media at that time. I was of the view that it was too early to reveal anything. 'Sir, many explosions have taken place and the larger plan of the terrorists is still unknown. We should not disclose our line of investigation as any information broadcast by the media will also be viewed by the terrorists,' I told him.

The CP agreed and while he walked towards his car, media personnel surrounded him and asked many questions. *Who is responsible for all this? The Indian Mujahideen has emailed the media; who are the members of this group? What kinds of explosives were used?*

'It is immaterial who takes the responsibility. Our job is to catch the actual perpetrators who have planted bombs and conspired to do so. The forensic team is examining the explosives used and its actual constituents will be ascertained by the Central Forensic Science Laboratory (CFSL), which may take some time. The Delhi Police Special Cell will be working on the cases,' the CP addressed the media on his way out. On his way, he sent a message to all the senior officers of the rank of DCP and above posted in field units, Special Cell, PCR and Crime Branch to reach the police headquarters by 10:30 p.m. for an emergency meeting.

On learning about the email that had been sent to the media houses, I requested the media personnel to share the same with the Special Cell. I also called the Special Cell office, informing them about the email and that we needed to track its source. 'Put a team of experts on this immediately. Also, call for a meeting at 11.30 p.m. at the Lodhi Road office with the entire team,' I told the Special Cell office.

I decided to go to the children's park where one of the bombs was defused. On Saturdays, the park is full of children and their parents. My thoughts raced to my own three children at home and I silently thanked God that these bombs were defused before they could explode.

After checking the park site, Sanjeev and I went to the Tilak Marg police station, where one of the defused bombs was kept. Mohan had also reached the police station with his team to examine the bomb. The examination revealed that each bomb was kept in a plastic bag. The bomb had a boat-shaped wooden casing that was filled with explosives and cycle ball bearings, and electronic detonators were also placed along with the explosives. The wooden casing had an outer iron covering (on explosion, the iron casing breaks and its pieces act as shrapnel). Holes were made in the casing, through which electric wires connecting the electronic detonator were brought out and connected to a quartz watch, which was attached to the casing using tape. The casing, along with explosive material and the detonator, was wrapped in plastic.

Mohan shared with everyone that the bombs were identical to those planted in Ahmedabad on 26 July and in Jaipur on 13 May that year.

These synchronized attacks in many parts of the country pointed to a large terror network that was well connected, had access to bombs and was able to work undetected so far. We had to stop them before they could strike again.

On the way to the Delhi Police headquarters, I started reading the email sent to the media by the terror group. It came with an attached PDF running into 13 pages. The sender of the email claimed sole responsibility for the serial blasts in Delhi. The email was titled 'Resolve to fight till the end'. The document started with the photos of the 2002 Gujarat riot victims with the caption 'Eye for an Eye: The Dust Will Never Settle Down'.[5] It was released by a group that went by the name Indian Mujahideen (IM).

I had so many questions. *Who is behind the group? How is it different from the other terror groups that have attacked in the past? Where does it originate?*

It was the fifth email from IM. The first one was sent on 23 November 2007 during the Uttar Pradesh (UP) serial blasts that targeted courts. IM was not known prior to that date. *This module seems to have grown to create havoc through such organized attacks.*

State Police forces and intelligence agencies across the country were unsure about the identity and origin of IM. One theory was that this group was actually the Students Islamic Movement of India (SIMI) and that IM derived its name by removing 'S' and 'I' from the abbreviation 'SIMI'. Some believed it to be part of the Harkat-ul-Jihad-al-Islami (HuJI), while others believed it to be part of the Lashkar-e-Taiba (LeT). However, the real nature or origin of the militant outfit was still a mystery at the time. There was a lot of information that the agencies did not have.

I brought to mind the origin and activities of these terror outfits so far to map out what we knew and if there were any leads that could be explored.

HuJI is an Islamic fundamentalist organization with the motto 'Movement of Islamic Holy War'. It was founded in 1979 in Karachi by Maulana Irshad Ahmed, Qari Saifullah Akhtar and Maulana Abdus Samad Sial during the Soviet–Afghan

---

[5]'Eye for an Eye: The Dust Will Never Settle Down', 'Indian Mujahideen in the Land of Hind', emailed to the media on 13 September 2008, New Delhi.

War (1979–89), and is theologically close to the Deoband school of thought. Its primary motive was to take volunteers to Afghanistan to help the rebels fight the Soviets. HuJI initially operated in Afghanistan. After the retreat of the Soviets, they started sending jihadis to J&K. By 1992, it had further expanded its operations to Bangladesh and was supported directly by Osama Bin Laden in this effort. It was banned in Bangladesh in 2005 and in India in 2006.

LeT was one of the largest active terror organizations in South Asia. It was said to be directly funded by Osama Bin Laden. They called themselves the 'Army of the Righteous' or the 'Army of the Pure' and aimed for the integration of J&K with Pakistan. The LeT imparts combat training to the young and encourages them to pick up arms and become militants for their cause. This organization was involved in several attacks on military and civilian targets in India. In 1988, it killed 23 Kashmiri pandits in the Wandhama massacre. In October 2005, it carried out multiple bomb blasts in Delhi and caused multiple blasts in Mumbai in July 2006, among many others. Ironically, on the surface, they run humanitarian activities and raise funds for charity (in schools, ambulances, mobile clinics, etc.).

SIMI was founded on 25 April 1977 in Aligarh, UP. It started out as a students' wing of the Jamaat-e-Islami Hind (JIH). SIMI's ideology promoted the restoration of 'khilafat' (caliphate), emphasizing on Muslim brotherhood (*ummah*) and the establishment of supremacy of Islam. They opposed the idea of secularism, democracy and nationalism. Keeping in view their anti-national activities, the Government of India had imposed a ban on them in 2001. On 10 April 2006, there was a split in SIMI on the grounds of ideology. The Dr Shahid Badar Falahi-led group followed moderate path, while the Safdar Nagori-led radical group decided to take violent action by radicalizing more and more youth, training them and then exhorting them to wage war against the State by causing explosions and killings. In March 2008, top leaders of the Nagori group including Safdar Nagori himself, were arrested by the Madhya Pradesh Police. The leadership of this group was then passed on to Abdul Subhan Qureshi, alias Tauqeer. In August 2008, the Gujarat Police arrested another set of SIMI members for causing explosions in July in the state. Subhan and Qayamuddin Kapadia, both leaders of SIMI, were in hiding thereafter. The Gujarat Police had come out with the theory that IM is nothing but SIMI.

Which terror group is IM or which group is it connected with? There must be links to larger terror organizations for it to be able to carry out such extensive bomb blasts. We had to connect these dots to unearth this terrorist group.

I read the email further. The second page had the IM logo, which was a globe with a book placed on top of it with two jihadis standing back to back carrying AK-series weapons. The third page started with the prayer in honour of the Almighty and His messenger Mohammad—'In the Name of Allah, The Most Beneficent, The Most Merciful.'

Coming to the main threat in the email, the writer shared that 'the intense, accurate and successive attacks like the one you will see exactly five minutes from now...NINE MOST POWERFUL SERIAL BOMBS BLASTS.'

The IM claimed that these explosions would take place five minutes after the email was sent out (the mail was sent at 6.27 p.m.). There were five explosions: four of them after the email was sent (between 6.30 p.m. to 6.35 p.m.), while one at Karol Bagh at 5.55 p.m., indicating something was amiss in its execution. Luckily, three explosive devices were timely detected in dustbins by the beat constables and were defused.

One bomb seemed to be unaccounted for. *Where was it?*

IM had claimed to have masterminded various explosions in many cities in the past. In this particular email, it claimed to have meticulously planned and executed explosions in Ahmedabad and Surat on 26 July 2008. Ahmedabad had seen a series of 23 bomb blasts (21 blasts took place in market areas and two blasts in cars parked in the hospital premises), killing 56 people and injuring more than 200, while the bombs in Surat failed to explode and were defused.

The email also stated that 'we are about to devastate your very first metropolitan centre, New Delhi, with nine bomb blasts, that are almost going to stop the "heart of India" from beating. By this attack, we intend to prove the ability and potential of IM to assault any city of India.'

The attacks seemed to have been meticulously planned and they were clearly trying to prove that their might could not be countered. The email stated:

> *This attack has now confirmed that all your attempts to stop our advance have failed and whatever false claims made about the crackdown of the terror modules...then which 'mastermind' executed today's attack? Which 'terror module' slapped your ugly face today?*

IM was trying to insinuate that the arrests made by different states in bomb blast cases were of innocent people and not of actual planners or bombers. IM was particularly upset with the arrests made by the Gujarat Police stating that if they had arrested the mastermind, then who was behind the Delhi blasts.

I stopped reading the email as I reached the headquarters by then. At 10.30 p.m., the top brass of the Delhi Police gathered in the PCR conference room located on the fourth floor of the Delhi Police headquarters at ITO in Central Delhi.

The CP spoke to everyone in the room and started by reviewing the condition of the injured and the arrangements made at the hospitals. He showed deep concern about the situation and said that unless the terrorists responsible for the blasts were identified and arrested, they could further wreak havoc in the city. Another cause of worry was that *Ramleelas*[6] would start after a fortnight, which would result in large gatherings in every nook and corner of the city. He emphasized that all the officers and policemen were required to reach out to the public, the resident welfare associations and the market associations to chalk out a joint strategy, take their help to install CCTV cameras wherever needed, place door frame metal detectors (DFMD) in all the markets and activate and use the 'eyes and ears scheme'[7] of the Delhi Police extensively.

I asked the district DCPs to carry out extensive enquiries in the city about anyone who purchased ammonium nitrate

---

[6]Ramleela is a street play that re-enacts the life of Rama and is organized across the country every year for 10 days during Dussehra.

[7]The 'eyes and ears scheme' was initiated by Delhi Police Chief Y.S. Dadwal on 18 January 2008. It aimed at developing criminal-and terrorist-related intelligence by involving people who spend most of their time on the roads, markets and colonies, viz., roadside vendors (*rehri patriwalas*), security guards (chowkidars), and people working at STD/ISD booths, cybercafés, petrol pumps, etc. Such individuals see people moving up and down throughout the day. Over a period, they are able to gather a lot of information that never reaches the operational levels of the police or in a limited manner. They are in a good position to spot suspicious activities and movements of individuals, particularly if someone leaves behind a bag or any unidentified object in a suspicious manner. Beat constables were directed to be in contact with such individuals on a day-to-day basis and were asked to organize at least one fortnightly meeting with them, while the station house officer (SHO) conducts such meetings once in a month, the ACP once in two months and the DCP once every quarter. A special helpline number, 1090, was assigned for this purpose so that they could give information directly to local police officers or to the helpline. This scheme has given excellent results in detecting live bombs, thereby saving many lives.

from the explosive shops (the shopkeepers selling explosives are required to maintain proper records of anyone who purchases the explosives) and about any recent bulk sale of quartz clocks. I also asked the district DCPs of South, Central and New Delhi (districts where the blasts had taken place) to collect and examine CCTV footages from the markets, metro stations and residential colonies. I asked the teams deployed at the hospitals to question all the injured before they were discharged. The identity verification of dead persons was also to be carried out quickly. (Sometimes terrorists themselves get injured or die in such blasts; this exercise is done to eliminate any such possibility.) I conveyed that the Special Cell would be coordinating with the district police, investigating agencies of other states and the central intelligence agencies to collate and share leads with them and follow those leads. With the procedure and plan of action set in motion, the meeting ended. I looked at the clock. It was 45 minutes to midnight.

After the meeting, I immediately left for our Lodhi Colony office for the 11.30 p.m. meeting. Most of the officers were still in the field, investigating the cases. The officers present were briefed about the decisions taken in the meeting held at the Delhi Police headquarters. Further course of action regarding the procurement of dump data of mobiles located at the blast sites, investigation of the source of emails sent by IM at various occasions, analysis of emails, questioning of auto drivers at the Karol Bagh blast site, coordination with districts and other states where explosions had taken place in the past, etc., were discussed. It was decided to hold a meeting at 11.30 a.m. the next day after all the officers returned from investigations at the sites. They were asked to work round the clock as time was of great essence or else the terrorists might strike again.

On my way back home, I resumed reading the email that

further made specific threats to anti-terror units of various states, politicians across party lines and media personnel. It seemed they believed that through such threats, the media would toe their lines and the police would stop arresting terrorists. They had perhaps underestimated the courage of the media and the policemen who would stand by their country.

Going back to the mail, it stated:

We, the Indian Mujahideen, ask Allah, the Almighty to accept from us these nine explosions which were planned to be executed in the holy month of Ramadan. We have carried out this attack in the memory of two most eminent Mujahids of India: Sayyed Ahmed Shaheed and Shah Ismail Shaheed (may Allah bestow His Mercy upon them) who had raised the glorious banner of Jihad against the disbelievers in this very city of Delhi. It is the great hard work and sacrifices of these visionary legends that shall always inspire us, Inshallah, to carry on the struggle and fight against the Kufr (disbelief) till our last breath.

Sayyed Ahmed Shaheed (referred to in the mail) was born in Rae Bareli, a part of the historical United Provinces of Agra and Oudh (now UP) in 1786. He desired to establish an Islamic State on the pattern of the early Caliphate in the Indian subcontinent and, possibly, in the rest of the world. He declared that he would wage jihad against the 'infidels'. He moved to Peshawar and with Shah Ismail Shaheed, started a jihadi movement with the help of tribal folks from Afghanistan. They were defeated by the Sikhs in the Battle of Balakot of 1831.

The mail further stated that: 'It is very sad to see the bad condition of your cyber forensics who have still failed to find out our technique of sending the "Message of Death".' The terrorists were gloating over their 'technique' and mocking the investigation agencies. I wondered what technique they were referring to that we were ignorant of. The mail concluded by stating,

> To end with, we have now proved to you that the more you trouble us, the more you will be troubled by us. This deadliest strike at Delhi once again makes it clear that our threats are not at all limited to mere words and with the will and Permission of Allah, the action is in front of your eyes...and by The Grace of Allah, there is no shortage of explosives or lack of manpower and we are extremely capable to shed your blood anywhere anytime. The battle has now begun and the dust will never settle down.

Their pride in their capability and determination to continue terror attacks was unsettling. *We must move faster than them. No more lives should be lost to this mindless terrorism.*

It was 1.30 at night when I finally hit the bed, contemplating on IM and how to crack the case of explosions. The words 'the battle has now begun and the dust will never settle down' were resounding in my ears. It was a challenge to the police and the nation itself. I had handled difficult cases in the past and had tremendous faith in the capabilities of my men. *The dust must be settled soon.*

2

AN 11-YEAR-OLD BALLOON BOY

14 September 2008, Sunday
(Five days before the Batla House shoot-out)

At around 2 a.m., my phone rang. It was Sanjeev. Referring to the email from IM the previous day, he said, 'Sir, SI Ravinder Kumar Tyagi[8] had written a letter to Yahoo asking them to retrieve the Internet Protocol (IP) address of the email sent by IM to the media. At around 10.30 p.m. yesterday, we got a reply from Yahoo that the Mahanagar Telephone Nigam Limited (MTNL), Mumbai, is the service provider for that particular IP address.'

'Did you find out which number is using that IP?' I asked.

'Yes, it is registered in the name of a power company in Chembur. The Mumbai Police went to check that address, but it turned out to be an open Wi-Fi.[9] They have seized the router for forensic analysis, but it may be a dead end if forensics doesn't reveal anything.'

'Keep following up with them on this. Have the requests

---

[8]A technology-savvy officer who had taken part in many important operations against terrorists and criminals.
[9]Wi-Fi is termed as open Wi-Fi when it can be logged into either without a password or with the general password provided by the service provider.

for dump data[10] of cell towers been sent to all the service providers?'

He confirmed that he had done it and had spoken personally to the service providers. I asked him to be ready next morning for a meeting along with the cyber cell in-charge SI Chhanda Sahejwani and SI Ravinder to discuss tracing of the previous four emails sent by IM.

After putting the phone down, I surmised that tracing the email was not getting the desired results. The Wi-Fi systems were recently introduced and a number of people either did not have password-protected Wi-Fi or did not change common passwords given by the service providers. This helped IM take advantage of open Wi-Fi systems.

3.00 a.m.

I was unable to get any sleep that night, as there was a lot going on in my mind about everything that needed to be done to ensure all the leads were covered. My phone rang again an hour later. Anand Mohan, DCP, New Delhi District (an IPS officer of the 1994 batch) was at the other end. 'Sir, sorry to call you so early in the morning. We have an eyewitness. An 11-year-old boy named Rahul, who sells balloons on Barakhamba Road, told the police that he saw two men getting down from an autorickshaw. One of them dropped a plastic bag into a nearby dustbin. Within 15 minutes, the dustbin exploded. According to Rahul, one of them had a long beard and was clad in a black outfit, possibly a kurta-pyjama. The other person was wearing a shirt and trousers, and was clean-shaven. Rahul is now at the Connaught Place police station. His family members have

---

[10]Whenever a call is made from or to a cell phone, its location is recorded to indicate which cell tower it is connected to. Dump data pertains to all calls made or received through that cell tower.

also come to the police station. A few representatives from a children's NGO and a psychiatrist are helping Rahul rebuild the chronology of events.'

'Excellent, Anand! He may provide some leads. Get the sketch of the suspects prepared with his help. We should also question auto drivers to see if anyone can give any leads about the duo. What about the questioning of the injured and arrangements at the hospitals?'

'Sir, we have made strong arrangements at Dr Ram Manohar Lohia Hospital, where the injured and dead were shifted from the explosion sites located in the New Delhi District. All the vehicles parked in the hospital premises have been thoroughly checked for bombs and explosives. Many VIPs are visiting the hospital.'

'Do you know who detected the bombs that didn't explode?'

'As soon as the call of the first explosion in Karol Bagh was received and Red Alert was sounded off in Delhi, maximum number of police officers moved out in the field.' There was excitement in his voice. 'They also followed it up with stakeholders of the "eyes and ears scheme". The beat officers were already in the field, as it was evening time. A 32-year-old vendor named Kundan spotted a package, wrapped in a black polythene bag and taped with black tape. It was kept in a garbage bin next to Regal Cinema. He immediately informed Beat Constable Suresh Kumar. Without wasting any time, Suresh ripped the timer from the package and rendered the bomb ineffective. At India Gate, a 20-year-old ragpicker, Krishna, found a similar packet inside a dustbin just outside the children's park. He immediately informed Beat Constable Jaivir, who pulled out the timer device attached to the package. The bomb at Central Park was detected by the two HCs Sanjay and Rajender just a few minutes before another bomb went off in the park.'

It was very brave of these men to risk their lives trying to rip off the bomb with bare hands. Some would perhaps call it foolish, but in my many years of service with the police department, I know that most men would not think of themselves or their families in moments such as these. They would dutifully take that risk if it meant saving lives. All these men were later rewarded by the commissioner.

I concluded the phone call by instructing Anand to obtain and examine the CCTV footages on priority. After the call ended, I closed my eyes and tried to catch some sleep.

At 3.45 a.m., I received another call from Alok Kumar, DCP, Central District (an IPS officer of the 1996 batch), 'Sir, many people have been questioned at the spot and all the injured have been too, but no one could tell anything worthwhile. Moolchand, the driver of an auto in which explosion took place, is not in a condition to give any statement yet. He will be questioned as soon as he is stable. Police teams have been deployed in the hospitals. CCTV footages are being retrieved from the markets and the metro stations.'

'Most of the explosive shops are located in Central and North districts. Please get all the explosive shops checked tomorrow early morning. We have to work fast to catch the terrorists. Time is running out. Please convey this to DCP North District also. We should identify where the materials were obtained from.'

I gave up on the hope of getting any sleep altogether that night. Getting out of bed quietly, I went outside the room. At around 4.00 a.m., DCP (South District) H.G.S Dhaliwal (an IPS officer of the 1997 batch), called to update me about the questioning of the people at the spot and in the hospitals. He reassured that strict arrangements have been made at the All India Institute of Medical Sciences (AIIMS) and other hospitals.

I made myself a cup of tea and spent the rest of the night, or rather early morning, planning the next steps. At around 7.00 a.m., I was ready to leave for work. I picked up the newspapers and read them in the car. There were a number of news items about the explosions. One of them highlighted the compensation package announced by the Delhi government. It had decided to give ₹5 lakh to the next of kin of the people killed in the explosion and ₹50,000 to the wounded. The government announced that the treatment of all persons impacted by this blast would be free of charge in both government and private hospitals.

One of the headlines read: '*Satta mili to sau din main POTA* (If we come to power, then POTA will be enacted within 100 days)': Advani.[11]

I recalled my meeting with Shri L.K. Advani in April 1998. He was the Union Home Minister of India at that time. Forty-two blasts had taken place during 1996–98 in and around Delhi. I was working as DCP (Crime) at that time. My team cracked those cases and 27 modules of the LeT were caught from all over India. He had called me as he wanted to congratulate the Crime Branch team. I, along with the then CP (Shri T.R. Kakkar), Union Home Secretary, Director IB and ACP Ravi Shankar met him in the Ministry of Home Affairs. During our discussion, Shri Advani talked about the inadequacy of existing laws in dealing with terrorism. He showed his resolve to handle terrorism with a strong hand and indicated that he would bring stricter laws to tackle it.

I had often felt that India needed a more comprehensive policy framework to tackle terrorism. There had been situational

---

[11]POTA (Prevention of Terrorism Act), an anti-terror law, was enacted by the Bharatiya Janata Party (BJP) government in 2002 and was later repealed by the United Progressive Alliance (UPA) government in 2004.

knee-jerk reactions to certain grave incidents in the past. But we needed something more consistent.

India has been facing insurgency problems in some of the North-eastern states since Independence and Naxalism in Central India since 1967. The late 1970s saw the emergence of Pakistan-backed terrorism in Punjab. While militants' actions intensified in number and impact, the intelligence and investigation agencies were reliant on very basic laws, such as the Indian Penal Code (IPC), The Explosive Substances Act, 1908, etc. To deal with terrorism-related investigation and prosecution, security agencies used existing legislations in an ad hoc manner. Often a need was felt for an overarching and exhaustive anti-terror legislation to be instituted specially for terrorism cases.

On 1 June 1984, Operation Blue Star was carried out by the Indian military within the Golden Temple in Amritsar, Punjab. The then PM, Mrs Indira Gandhi, had given orders to the military to enter the temple premises and bring out the Sikh extremist leader Jarnail Singh Bhindranwale and his armed militant group. The entry of armed forces inside the Golden Temple hurt the religious sentiments of common Sikhs and it resulted in the assassination of Mrs Gandhi by two of her Sikh bodyguards on 31 October that year.

As a knee-jerk reaction, in May 1985, the central government approved the Terrorist and Disruptive Activities (Prevention) Act (TADA), which was a precursor to POTA. It was hoped that this law would be efficient in dealing with anti-terror cases.

TADA stipulated that the confessions before police officers (of and above the rank of superintendent) constituted as significant evidence and was permissible in the court of law. It also stipulated provision for pretrial detention and had very strict rules for bail.

TADA proved to be an effective tool in the hands of the police dealing with terrorism. However, some human rights activists and non-governmental organizations (NGOs) started opposing TADA alleging that few of its aspects infringed on the fundamental rights and international human rights treaties. They also alleged that it was extensively abused by the police. In 1995, the government allowed TADA to lapse due to grave political opposition on its misuse.

Meanwhile, Pakistan-supported jihadi terrorism started taking an ugly turn, resulting in some of the most dastardly attacks, viz., the October 2001 attack on the J&K Assembly and the December 2001 attack on the Parliament. The BJP government wasted no time in bringing a new POTA in 2002 to effectively deal with terrorism. Shri Advani was the then Home Minister.

In 2004, as soon as the UPA formed the government at the Centre, POTA was repealed on the grounds similar to that of TADA. Some of the provisions pertaining to acts of terror were included in the Unlawful Activities (Prevention) Act (UAPA), 1967. However, UAPA, even after new amendments, was a relatively weaker act in tackling terrorism. It was in this background that Shri Advani had made the statement about bringing POTA within a month if BJP comes to power, as mentioned earlier. I wondered how the central government would react to this statement.

At around 8.00 a.m., the PCR informed us that the explosions had resulted in the death of 22 people and caused injury to 131. Some of the injured were still in a critical condition. I asked the PCR to send a hospital-wise list of the casualties and the injured. This piece of information was crucial to the investigation.

I called the CP and briefed him about the leads and

developments in the case. He emphasized that IM had been causing explosions, month after month, resulting in huge loss of life and creating fear in the minds of the people. 'We must deploy all resources and stretch ourselves to the core to apprehend them and stop their dastardly acts. Karnal, you have experience of solving difficult cases in the past. You must put your best men and solve this immediately,' he said.

'Sir, all the officers are working round the clock and we will try our best to solve the mystery of IM and these blasts,' I assured him.

11.30 a.m.

We, the Special Cell team, had a meeting at our Lodhi Colony office at 11.30 a.m. As mentioned earlier, Alok had to cut short his family trip to Vaishno Devi to resume his duties.

'How was your trip, Alok?' I asked him with a subdued sense of guilt since I had to cancel his leave.

'It was good, sir. The family had been waiting for this trip, so were happy that we could actually see Vaishno Devi. It's okay, sir, if it was a short trip,' replied Alok with a smile on his face.

'I am glad you are back; we need all hands on deck for this one.'

'Sir, we are always ready to serve our country, nothing is more important than this.' I really appreciated the commitment of the team and I knew that every officer felt the same way.

I took stock of the status of the investigation. There were two eyewitnesses who could throw some light on the terrorists. One was Rahul, the balloon-seller, who had seen two suspects and the other was Moolchand, the auto driver, who was seriously injured and still unfit to give a statement. The portraits of two of the terrorists were being prepared by the New Delhi district with the help of Rahul. The tasks of checking the shops selling explosives in Delhi and getting the CCTV footages were done by the district police. Dump data requests had been made to mobile-service providers by the Special Cell and the records were expected by 16 September. Email tracing and information exchange with other states and the central intelligence agencies were done by the Special Cell.

I asked Ravinder about the investigation being carried out in email tracing and if there was any possibility of getting clues through it.

'Sir, the first email was sent to the media by IM at the time of explosions in Lucknow, Faizabad and Varanasi courts in UP on 23 November 2007.'

Ravinder immediately collected the header of the email ID guru_alhindi@yahoo.fr and found that the alleged email was generated from an IP address that belonged to a cybercafé in Shakarpur in east Delhi. His team then went to investigate the cybercafé and met its owner. There were 11 networked computers in the café. The team checked the logs to ascertain the computer used for sending the email. The owner was asked to give the identity of the person who had used that computer, but he could not recall anything. He handed over the register of visitors. It only had information about the duration and time of the computers' usage and the amount charged from the user. It did not have any record of the identity of the users. The team was furious, as it was mandatory for all cybercafés to keep the ID proofs of all the users. However, it was found that no ID proofs were maintained after 29 July 2007. The hard disks of all the 11 computers were seized and were examined in the cyber lab.

Recording the identity of cybercafé users may appear mundane and of no value to many, but here this could have been a crucial step in the investigation. It was frustrating but nothing could be done then. We had to find something else that would lead us to them.

I then asked Chhanda, an expert in cyber forensics who had accompanied the team in many outstation operations, if anything came up through the cyber analysis. She explained, 'The person who sent the email appears to be an expert in computers. The first thing he did was to change the clock settings of the computer. After his work was done, he restored the clock settings. He did it so that the logs get jumbled, making analysis of his activities difficult. To begin with, he created a new email ID, guru_alhindi@yahoo.fr. The file (Modify.doc) attached with the email was not created in the cybercafé. He had downloaded it from a Kingston pen drive, which he must have brought with him. The mounting time of this pen drive, was at 03:42:36 on 1 January 2007 (as per the tampered time of the computer, 1 January 2007 03:42:36 is equivalent to 23 November 2007 13:18:00). The sender did not access any website or use any other email during the period of surfing the internet. No further clue could be found that could help in tracing the sender of the email.'

Ravinder further intimated that the second email was sent by IM on 14 May 2008, claiming responsibility for the Jaipur blasts that took place on 13 May that year. This email originated from a cybercafé located at Sahibabad in UP. The owner of this cybercafé was also not maintaining records of people using the computers installed therein, so it wasn't of much help either. During the investigation, it was revealed that the modus operandi adopted by the sender of this email was the same as that of the first email.

Ravi shared that the third email with the ID alarbi_gujarat@ yahoo.com by IM was sent at the time of the Gujarat blasts on 26 July 2008. This email was found to be generated from

Mumbai through an open Wi-Fi. This investigation was done by the Mumbai Police. After sending the email, the sender deleted his mail trail from the Wi-Fi volatile memory (contents stored in a volatile memory are lost as soon as power supply is stopped). It clearly established that senders of emails from Delhi and Mumbai had a good understanding of computer systems. Further, on 23 August 2008, another email from the ID alarbi.alhindi@gmail.com was sent by IM to the electronic and print media. But email tracing could not give any leads in the investigation.

'Mohan, the name "guru" has appeared in the first two emails originating from Shakarpur and Sahibabad. Try to locate whether this name appeared in any interrogation reports.' I instructed Mohan, an expert in building human intelligence.

I further asked Alok and Sanjeev to examine all the emails and share their thoughts.

'IM claimed responsibility for the Gujarat blasts of 26 July 2008 and the Gujarat Police had arrested some SIMI members in the blast cases. Any leads from them?' I enquired.

Alok said that Ravi's and Sanjeev's teams had visited Gujarat in the past and interacted with the Gujarat Police. He briefly summarized their reports.

Twenty-three explosions had taken place in Ahmedabad between 6.30 p.m. and 7.45 p.m. on 26 July 2008, which had resulted in the death of 56 people and injured 240. Three bombs were defused. Significantly, two blasts had occurred in vehicles in two hospitals where several victims of the explosions were being rushed to, thus resulting in more deaths and injuries. The timing of blasts at these hospitals was carefully planned to cause maximum casualties.

The Surat Police had recovered another 29 bombs from various parts of the city between 28 July and 31 July 2008. The materials used in the bombs in Surat were similar to those used in Ahmedabad, except that the timing devices were made using integrated circuits rather than watches. The places for planting bombs in Ahmedabad City were selected by terrorists with the intention of inciting communal tension. The places of planting and timings set for bombs in Surat were selected to cause maximum casualties and breakdown of the economy, as diamond workers and an elevated highway were targeted.

Two Maruti WagonR cars with live bombs were detected in Surat. It was later found that these cars had been stolen from Navi Mumbai in July 2008. The Mumbai Police picked up a number of car thieves and interrogated them but was not able to get any significant information from them.

On 15 August 2008, the Gujarat Police, after investigations, arrested 10 people having allegiance to SIMI. They had also located the hideouts of the terrorists, and one of them was in Ahmedabad. According to them, Mufti Abu Bashir, Qayamuddin and Subhan stayed in that house to plan and execute the explosions in Gujarat. While Abu Bashir was arrested by the police, Qayamuddin and Subhan were on the run. The Gujarat Police had concluded Subhan to be the head of IM, that Subhan and Qayamuddin had planned and executed the blasts in Gujarat and that IM was nothing but camouflaged SIMI.

Sanjeev informed us that the Special Cell teams had also visited the Jaipur blast sites. The nine synchronized explosions took place within 15 minutes at seven locations on 13 May 2008. A tenth bomb was detected and defused. The first two blasts occurred at Manak Chowk at 7.10 p.m. The crowd started running towards Johri Bazar when two more explosions happened near the National Handloom Centre. This blocked one of the exits from the market and people then ran towards

Chandpol Bazar and Tripolia Bazar, where successive blasts resulted in 64 fatalities and another 216 being injured. The bombs were planted on bicycles. The Jaipur Police had suspected that the explosions had similarities with those in Varanasi and Hyderabad. At both the places, some HuJI (Bangladeshi) terrorists were caught and therefore the Jaipur Police suspected the role of HuJI in the Jaipur blasts as well. However, after the arrest of a few SIMI members on 15 August 2008 by the Gujarat Police, the Rajasthan Police also started investigating the role of SIMI in the Jaipur blasts. The Rajasthan Police, with the help of the UP Police, arrested SIMI leader Shahbaz Hussain from Lucknow on 25 August 2008. Besides him, six more people were arrested under the UAPA.

Mohan shared with us that on 28 August, the central intelligence agency had shared three mobile numbers (9712398204, 9714552899 and 9724764196) which were used by IM while planning and executing explosions in Gujarat. They were activated on 14 July and were switched off on the day of the blasts, i.e., on 26 July 2008. Mohan's team analysed the call data records (CDRs) of these mobile phones and found that one of these numbers (9714552899) was in Delhi between 17 July and 23 July 2008, and thereafter it returned to Gujarat. It was located in the Jamia Nagar area during this period.

Mohan showed the call records as he explained that these three numbers were working in closed loop and had no incoming or outgoing calls from or to any other mobile number outside the group except one incoming call on 9712398204 from a BSNL east UP number 9415835341. This call was for the duration of one second.[12] Generally such disconnected calls do not raise suspicion; however, Mohan, to be absolutely sure

---

[12]When a phone call is disconnected without accepting it, the call data records show such a call to be of one-second duration.

that this number was not from the terror group, analysed it further. The usual location of this number was in Lucknow (which could mean that the person who used this number resides in Lucknow). However, when he made a call to the number linked to the terrorist, his location was in Mumbai. Further, this number did not travel to Gujarat. It was found to be registered in the name of Dr Shahnawaj and was connected to numerous numbers from Mumbai, Punjab and other states. In Delhi, it was in regular touch with 9811004309, the location of which was found to be in Zakir Nagar.

Subscriber details of the Delhi mobile number 9811004309 was collected and it was found that initially it was a prepaid number in the name of Mirza Shadab Beg, and was activated on 1 April 2007. Mirza Shadab Beg could not be traced. This number was subsequently changed from prepaid to postpaid on 11 August 2008 (after the Gujarat blasts) in the name of Mohd. Atif Ameen, whose address was registered at Flat no. 108, L-18, Batla House, Zakir Nagar, Delhi.

The connectivity of this number with the terrorists' numbers was remote as usually criminals and terrorists do not use postpaid numbers. However, since one of the three numbers used by IM was in Delhi between 17 July and 23 July and was located in Jamia Nagar, and the location of 9811004309 was in Zakir Nagar, which was adjacent to Jamia Nagar, the number yielded suspicion and was taken in for observation. We were scrutinizing every call, every number that fell in the radar of suspicion and trying to connect the dots.

I appreciated Mohan's analytical work on the phone numbers and asked him to continue monitoring and analysing the calls. I also asked him to take the mobile phones of all the closely connected numbers on observation.

Sanjeev added that his team had obtained the dump data of

the cell phone tower locations of all the blast sites in Gujarat and Rajasthan, but analysis did not yield any result. He was of the opinion that the terrorists were not carrying the mobile phones with them while planting the bombs, else analysis would have led to some clues. 'Good observation, Sanjeev. However, we should not leave any thread unexplored. Thus, we can use this data and analyse it with the dump data of Delhi blast locations to check for any clues,' I said.

I asked Ravi to compare the explosive devices used in Jaipur, Ahmedabad, Surat, Karnataka and Delhi. He had details of all except Karnataka. He requested that to expedite the matter, we would need information from the Intelligence Bureau (IB). I told him that I would coordinate and procure it from IB and pass it on to him.

Finally, I encouraged everyone to devote their full time to investigating the cases, 'We have to solve this before they strike again.'

I requested the central intelligence agency to provide the interrogation reports of all those arrested by the Gujarat Police. Request was also made to send the details of explosive devices used in the Karnataka blasts on 25 July 2008.

9.00 p.m.

Alok (DCP Central District) called me and apprised that the condition of the auto driver, Moolchand, had stabilized and he also shared with the police that a young boy of about 24 had hired his auto from the bus stand on Mathura Road near the Nizamuddin Police Station. The youth was carrying a bag and had asked to be taken to Patel Nagar via Gaffar Market (Karol Bagh), where he had some work. When the auto reached Karol Bagh, the boy asked the driver to stop near a tree. He told the driver that he was going to a mobile shop and would return shortly. He asked him to take care of his bag kept in the auto. The youth was carrying a cap in his hand. When he didn't return in 10–15 minutes, the driver came out of his auto to look for him. As he paced around 10–15 feet away from his auto, there was a huge explosion behind him. He fell down and got injured. He said that he would be able to help build a portrait of that youth.

'Good work, Alok! Get the portrait prepared at the earliest,' I conveyed to him before disconnecting the phone.

◆

15 September 2008,
(Four days before the Batla House shoot-out)

10.00 a.m

A journalist informed me that he had got some statements of the persons caught by the Gujarat and Rajasthan Police. I requested him to immediately forward the same on my email.

10.30 a.m.

I headed to the CP's office and apprised him about the outcome of the investigation so far. I told him that I had had a telephonic conversation with the head of CFSL, who informally confirmed that our guess about the use of ammonium nitrate in the explosives was correct, and that the formal report would take some time. Joint CP Ranges[13] intimated that portraits were being prepared with the help of Rahul and Moolchand. CCTV footages were being obtained from various places and enquiry from explosive shops and further enquiry about the persons who purchased ammonium nitrate was being done expeditiously.

---

[13]An officer heading a range. A group of two or three districts constitutes a range.

5.00 p.m.

After getting statements of the accused, arrested in Gujarat, from the Central Intelligence and the journalist, I was absorbed in reading them to understand the activities of SIMI and its connection with IM. The statements in brief brought out that:

All those arrested by the Gujarat Police were members of SIMI (Safdar Nagori faction). Except Abu Bashir, who hails from Azamgargh, all others are from Gujarat, mainly from Ahmedabad and Vadodara. The Safdar Nagori-led radical group was keen to take violent action by radicalizing more and more youth, training them and then exhorting them to wage war against the State by causing explosions and killings.

SIMI (Safdar Nagori) organized many training camps across India in order to get the youth ready for jihad. Beginning from August 2007, these camps were organized in Dharwar (Karnataka), Indore and Khandwa (Madhya Pradesh), Vagamon (Kerala) and Panchmahal (Gujarat). Nagori himself attended all the training camps. He along with Abu Bashir (arrested by the Gujarat Police for his involvement in the Gujarat blasts), Subhan and Qayamuddin (both wanted in the Gujarat blasts) gave speeches on jihad. They also resolved that jihad would be done to fight the cause of Muslims, to punish the persons behind the Babri Masjid demolition and the Gujarat riots, to take assistance for jihad from the outside world and efforts to be made to contact the Taliban. Participants were also imparted training on physical fitness and the handling of weapons.

The intelligence agencies got wind of the activities of the Safdar group and top leadership including Safdar Nagori were arrested in March 2008 by the Madhya Pradesh Police. The leadership of SIMI was then passed on to Abdul Subhan and Qayamuddin Kapadia. Subhan knew some of the IM members in Mumbai. He contacted them seeking its support in jihad. The IM group told him to provide logistic support as IM was planning something big in Gujarat. Subhan introduced them to Qayamuddin, who provided logistic support to IM in Gujarat.

The interrogation reports made it absolutely clear that SIMI and IM were distinct entities. Only two persons (Subhan and Qayamuddin) in SIMI could reveal the identity of the members of IM, and these two persons were on the run. Somehow they needed to be caught. Tracing the thief who stole the cars used in the Gujarat blasts would also prove to be a useful lead and since the cars were stolen from Navi Mumbai, the Mumbai Police was working on that.

The Special Cell and the district police teams were working indefatigably day and night, deploying informers, questioning various people, conducting enquiries at various places, conducting raids in multiple states, scientifically analysing the cell phone records and CCTV data, and doing technical surveillance in order to get a breakthrough.

3

DEEP DIVING INTO THE PAST

16 September 2008
(Three days before the Batla House shoot-out)

The day started with a meeting of the senior officers with the CP wherein I briefed him about the progress being made in the investigation. Joint CP Ranges shared their updates on the investigation being done by the officers posted in the ranges. CCTV footages were being reviewed for potential clues. There were about 174 shops in Delhi wherein explosives were readily available. The list of people who had purchased ammonium nitrate from these outlets had been obtained and antecedents of them were being verified by sending teams to various states. Portraits of the suspects were in their final stages of completion and there was a plan to circulate the same through the media by the evening. All those injured in the blasts had been questioned and their antecedents had been checked, but no one was found having a suspicious background. Almost 72 hours had passed and though we had no substantial results, we were in the process of linking the missing pieces. The CP stressed the need for coordinated investigation so that better results could be obtained.

I went to the Special Cell office and called for a meeting in the evening to ensure everyone was brought up to speed with the findings of the investigation. This would make connecting the dots easier, as everyone was working on different aspects of the case. Alok, Ravi, Sanjeev and Mohan, too, were part of this meeting.

Sanjeev had analysed the emails to get a deeper understanding of IM. He believed that there were irrefutable evidences through emails to prove that those sending these emails were part of IM and were actually responsible for the explosions. They were definitely not pranksters!

We started following the emails one by one and juxtaposed them with the corresponding blasts. The first email was sent during the UP court blasts on 23 November 2007. The explosions took place between 1.03 p.m. and 1.32 p.m. The email was sent at 1.18 p.m. The person had gone to a cybercafé carrying the email prepared beforehand on a pen drive indicating that the email document was prepared much before the explosions took place. The second email was sent on 14 May 2008, the day after the Jaipur blasts. The email had an attached video clip of the bomb on a bicycle with frame no 129489 placed near Kotwali in Jaipur. This clip could not have been with anyone except those who had actually planted the bombs in Jaipur. The third email was sent on 26 July 2008 at 6.40 p.m., while explosions in Ahmedabad took place between 6.30 p.m. and 7.45 p.m. The timing of the email was crucial in establishing that the Ahmedabad blasts were executed by IM. The fourth email was sent by IM on 23 August 2008, after the Gujarat Police did a press conference on 15 August about solving the cases of the Gujarat explosions. The email started with three photographs. The first photograph, with the caption 'Weapons of mass destruction' depicted several prepared and unexploded explosive devices, with blue and red wrappers, used in Gujarat. The second photograph, captioned 'Our favourite toys', was of two parked cars. The third photograph, captioned 'The cars that devastated you', was of two cars (before the blasts, with unexploded bombs), which had later exploded in Ahmedabad. These photographs could be available only with the perpetrators of the blasts and not with someone else claiming responsibility. The fifth email was sent during the Delhi blasts on 13 September 2008. The timings of the emails synchronized with the timings of the blasts and were proof enough that there was indeed a group called Indian Mujahideen, or IM, and that they were responsible for blasts in UP, Jaipur, Gujarat and Delhi.

Sanjeev stated, 'IM has also claimed responsibility for other blasts such as the one in Delhi that took place on 29 October 2005, three days prior to Diwali.'

I was posted in the Special Cell as Joint CP during that period. Delhi was in a festive mood. Dussehra was celebrated on 12 October, while Jumu'atul-Wida, the last Friday in the month of Ramadan before Eid-ul-Fitr, was on 28 October. Dhanteras was to be celebrated on 29 October and Diwali was on 1 November. On the auspicious day of Dhanteras, it is customary for Hindus to purchase jewellery and household items, among other things. Markets are extremely crowded during this day. I had left our ITO office to go to our Lodhi Colony office at 5.30 p.m. While I was on my way, I received a call from the PCR that a blast had taken place in the Paharganj market, near the New Delhi Railway Station at 5.38 p.m. The Delhi Police headquarters had sounded a Red Alert. I asked the Special Cell teams to immediately reach the spot.

By the time I reached, the local police, the PCR vehicles and locals had acted swiftly shifting the injured to nearby hospitals and cordoning off the area. The explosive device was planted in a two-wheeler that was parked outside a medical shop, M.S.

Medicos. When the bomb exploded, it tore through the shop and struck the popular street-food eatery next door. Several people lost their lives, while many others were injured.

During this time, the PCR further informed us about explosions and a fire at the Sarojini Nagar Market and another explosion in a bus in Govindpuri. I asked the then DCP (Special Cell) Ashok Chand to immediately send teams to the other sites and also to the hospitals where the injured were rushed to. Questioning the injured was crucial. Dr K.K. Paul, who was the then CP, asked me to meet him at the Sarojini Nagar Market. We both visited the market together. The Sarojini Nagar blast took place at 6.00 p.m. The bomb exploded close to a vendor who was using gas cylinders, which as a result triggered multiple explosions and led to an eruption of a fire in the surrounding shops. More than half a dozen commercial establishments and vehicles parked close to these shops were also damaged.

There was another blast in Govindpuri. Around 35–40 people were travelling in a bus and the conductor of the bus noticed a suspicious polybag. On asking around, he discovered that the bag did not belong to any of the passengers onboard. The passengers recalled that a suspicious-looking man had boarded the bus. He had refused to buy a ticket and it was he who had left the bag behind. Acting quickly, the driver and conductor alerted the passengers and asked them to step out of the bus. The explosion took place when the conductor was throwing the bag out of the bus. The promptness of the conductor saved many lives, although he and the driver were severely injured.

All these explosions resulted in the death of 62 people and caused injuries to around 210 people. The conductor of the bus had seen the suspicious-looking man and based on his input, a portrait of the suspect was made and circulated to the media. The Special Cell teams were working hard to crack the case when on 10 November 2005, Shri Nehchal Sandhu, the then additional director of IB who was posted in J&K, called and intimated that IB had kept a Thuraya satellite phone under observation. This phone was used by Abu Al Kama, head of the LeT in J&K. He had spoken to one Tariqe Ahmad Dar (TAD) on Dar's mobile number. These conversations were pertaining to the Delhi blasts of 29 October 2005.

After the blast, TAD received a message from Abu Huzefa, second-in-command of the LeT in J&K, to disown the responsibility of the Delhi blasts, as there was tremendous pressure on Pakistan and that the international community would stop earthquake relief if Pakistan was found to be associated with or helping the terror activities. TAD called the Kashmir News Agency (KNA) on behalf of the LeT and told them that the LeT was not behind the Delhi blasts. TAD also called up BBC and repeated the same message with the assumed name Abu Haneefa. Further, during a conversation, TAD told Abu Al Kama that some markets in Delhi had CCTV installed, but the blast sites had no CCTVs. He also communicated that all the four persons who had gone for causing explosions in Delhi had returned safely to Kashmir and they were ready to repeat the similar act again.

TAD had a history of being arrested by the local police in April 2005 when 70,000 Saudi riyal and a hand grenade were recovered from him. He was released on bail after a few days.

Shri Sandhu wanted the Special Cell team to be sent to Kashmir urgently. However, a team headed by Inspector Govind Sharma was already stationed in Srinagar for another important investigation. I asked Ashok, who had supervised and cracked many complicated cases while he was posted in the Crime Branch and the Special Cell, and Sanjeev to immediately activate this team. With the help of IB, TAD was arrested by the Special Cell team and brought to Delhi the very next day.[14] On further investigation, terror-funding transactions to TAD were also established. A person named Rafeeq was arrested for the Govind Puri blast. It goes to the credit of the conductor of the bus that the portrait prepared with his help absolutely matched with that of Rafeeq.

On examining all the facts of the Delhi blasts that took place during Diwali, it was concluded that these were indeed masterminded by the LeT. Abu Huzefa was later killed in an encounter with Mohan's team, while Abu Al Kama shifted base from J&K to Pakistan. Some other suspects could not be caught, as they, too, had shifted to Pakistan. I found it hard to believe that IM was responsible for those blasts. *There must be some ulterior motive of IM in claiming responsibility for the blasts which were executed by LeT or it is possible that the IM itself is associated with the LeT. Which other blasts have they claimed responsibility for?*

Sanjeev continued with his findings, 'Then IM also took responsibility of the Varanasi blasts that took place on 7 March 2006.'

The Varanasi blast of 2006 had shook the holy city like never before. The Sankat Mochan Temple in Varanasi was established by Goswami Tulsidas in the early sixteenth century. It is believed that devotees of Lord Hanuman who visit the temple regularly will receive special blessings from him. Every Tuesday and Saturday, a large number of devotees offer prayers here. On 7 March 2006, the queue was longer and the gathering was larger than usual. A large number of students had come to pray before their exams and there was also a wedding function at the temple. At around 6.20 p.m., a powerful bomb that was

---

[14]He was arrested by the local police in the past and was released on bail. So he was out from jail when this incident happened.

placed in a black cloth bag hanging from a tree near one of the temple gates exploded, causing many casualties. Almost at the same time, another blast took place at the waiting room of the Varanasi Railway Station. A third bomb was found in a black cloth bag in the Gowdhulia market and was defused by the police. A total of 28 people were killed and 101 injured in these blasts.

Forensic analysis of the defused bomb revealed the use of RDX. The wall clock of Samay brand was used as a timer and the explosive was placed in a pressure cooker. Two days later, a lesser-known group named Lashkar-e-Kahar took responsibility of these explosions. Abdullah Jabbar, the spokesperson for the group, reached out to a news agency in Srinagar and warned that similar blasts will follow in other cities. They said they would stop only when the government stopped its 'catch-and-kill' campaign in J&K.

In April 2006, the UP Police arrested six terrorists belonging to HuJI for causing these blasts. Thinking out loud, I said, 'These blasts were caused by HuJI. A number of suspects could not be identified and traced. If IM is claiming that Varanasi blasts were caused by them, then they may be connected to HuJI.'

'Yes, sir, it is possible that IM could be connected with HuJI. They are also claiming the 7/11 Mumbai train blasts of 2006,' Sanjeev added.

'Ravi, your team had worked on these blasts. What do you think?' I asked.

Ravi then gave us a rundown of the Mumbai train blasts. On 11 July 2006, it was a usual day at the Church Gate railway station—the heavy rush of daily commuters rushing back to their homes. Local trains on the Western Line of the suburban train network were packed. Between 6.24 p.m. and 6.30 p.m., seven powerful explosions took place in seven different trains at different stations, killing 209 commuters and injuring more than 700. The Improvised Explosive Devices (made using RDX) were kept in pressure cookers in first-class compartments. The Maharashtra Police ATS (Anti-Terrorism Squad) investigated the case and concluded that the terror attack was methodically planned by the LeT with the help of SIMI. Fifteen Pakistani nationals who had come to plant bombs had escaped to Pakistan after the blasts, while 13 SIMI persons were arrested and put to trial.

'Though IM is claiming that it caused these explosions in which members of the LeT, HuJI and SIMI were caught, it has explicitly stressed that the group is totally Indian, and it has no connection with HuJI, the LeT and ISI (Inter-Services Intelligence) of Pakistan,' Sanjeev added.

We now had all the data related to several blasts in the country in the past and it was staring at us like a jigsaw puzzle.

With an understanding of all the data that we had collectively found, I believed that the claim of these blasts by IM did not fit in well. The UP Police had arrested the terror group HuJI in some of the UP blast cases, while the Mumbai and Delhi police had found involvement of the LeT in the 7/11 Mumbai blasts and the 29/10 Delhi blasts. Some of the people who were involved in these blasts could not be identified. They could be from IM, or the LeT, or HuJI. But, why was IM claiming that HuJI or ISI or LeT had no role in these blasts? Was IM doing it at the instructions of the ISI as a strategy to deny Pakistan's role in terrorist activities in India? After the 9/11 Twin Tower attack in the United States (US), the United Nations (UN) turned on the heat on nations to seriously counter terrorism and terror financing. Any support given to terrorist activities, actively or passively, would result in serious action from the UN. The Financial Action Task Force (FATF) had also started monitoring the implementation of anti-terror mechanism in each nation. Therefore, it seemed to be in the interest of Pakistan/ISI to delink itself with the blasts in India so as not to attract international ire.

Sanjeev added, 'IM, in the last two emails, has claimed that it is not associated with SIMI. The Gujarat Police and the Mumbai Police had arrested SIMI members in bomb explosions in Gujarat and Mumbai respectively. The arrests had further given useful leads. IM may be diverting the focus of the investigating agencies.'

I agreed with Sanjeev that IM was trying to gaslight the investigation. Then, I turned to Mohan, 'Your team has extensively worked on HuJI. Can you enlighten us if anything suggests that HuJI had any connections with IM?'

Mohan said that in May 2008, his team had arrested a HuJI militant Abdur Rehman and after his interrogation, a person named Babu Bhai (he was in UP jail) was brought on remand. Babu Bhai, alias Jalaluddin Molla, was arrested on 23 June 2007 by the Special Task Force (STF) of the UP Police based on information provided by the central intelligence agency at the Lucknow railway station while he was deboarding a train coming from Kolkata. He was an active member of HuJI and was involved in radicalizing the youth and in transporting them for terror training to Pakistan. He also carried RDX from Bangladesh to different places in India. He claimed to have supplied RDX to a person named Guru, alias Rocky, in Delhi.

Ah, Guru! The name rang a bell.

'Mohan, one Guru is also the sender of first two emails of IM. Could this be connected? Tell us more about Babu Bhai's interrogation. We may find it useful in understanding the HuJI network in India,' I interjected.

Mohan elaborated that Babu Bhai was a resident of Billipara

village in West Bengal. He travelled to Bangladesh in 1984 to study in Jamia Rehmania Madrasa, Dhaka. Sometime in 1993–94, he met Asif Raza Khan in the madrasa. Asif tried to motivate him to join jihad and to fight against the Hindu fundamentalists who had demolished Babri Masjid and committed atrocities on the Indian Muslims.

After the completion of his education, Babu Bhai returned to Kolkata. Towards the end of 2000, Asif met Babu Bhai again and gave him the job of a delivery man and caretaker in his shoe godown.

Asif soon radicalized Babu Bhai and motivated him to go to Pakistan for arms and combat training. In March 2001, Babu Bhai crossed over to Bangladesh, where he met Asif and Qamar, alias Nata (head of HuJI Bangladesh). Qamar got a Bangladeshi passport made for him in the name of Zameel, as a resident of Murli near Jessore and arranged air tickets from Dhaka to Islamabad, Pakistan.

He was taken to a HuJI training camp at Kotri in Pakistan-occupied Kashmir (PoK). The camp housed 24 trainees from Malaysia, Philippines, South Africa and Pakistan. He was the lone Indian in the camp. They were imparted extensive training in the handling of arms and ammunition and various types of explosives.

On Fridays, a few Pakistani officials would visit the camp for an hour to interact with the trainees. They impressed upon the trainees the need to effectively use this training for protecting Islam and destroying its enemies.

After the completion of training, Babu Bhai was escorted to the Islamabad airport, where he was lodged in one of the rooms that was frequently used by Pakistani officials. He was kept there for three days as arrangements for his travel were not in place. During his stay at the airport, many Pakistani officials interacted with him and motivated him to make the best use of his training. They instigated him to cause maximum damage to the public property and to the citizens of India. The fact that he had gone to the training camp in PoK and successfully made it back to India, made it evident that an extensive network of terrorists was established in Bangladesh and Pakistan. Terrorists from various countries were undergoing training in PoK and the whole operation was done with the blessings and support of Pakistani officials.

After returning to Kolkata, Babu Bhai continued to work in Asif's office. During this period, Qamar and Asif's brother Amir also visited the office. Subsequently, in July 2001, Asif and his group kidnapped Partha Pratim Roy Burman, the owner of Khadim Shoes in Kolkata. Partha was only released after a heavy ransom was paid to the kidnappers.

Asif went to Agra to kidnap the owner of a departmental store, but was arrested by the Delhi Police. On the basis of the disclosure of Asif, a raid was conducted by the police at Babu Bhai's house. However, he managed to escape and remained in hiding for almost two years. He came to know later that Asif died during an encounter with the Gujarat Police.

Towards the end of 2003, he was called by Qamar to meet him in Dhaka, where he met Amir, Asif's brother. Amir motivated him to recruit more Indian Muslim youth for proper training in Pakistan. He escorted many people to Bangladesh for terror training. One of them was Guru, whom he escorted for training in August/September 2004.

On numerous occasions, Babu Bhai carried explosives from Dhaka to different destinations in India. He also delivered 20 kg of RDX to Guru at Gate No.1 Jama Masjid in August 2005.

On 6 June 2007, Qamar asked Babu Bhai to proceed to Lucknow, where Guru would meet him and hand over timers, detonators, etc., which, in turn, were to be handed over to Hafiz Naushad. On 7 June, he boarded the train from Kolkata to Lucknow, but before he could get off at his destination, Babu Bhai was arrested by the police. He was unaware of the whereabouts of Guru, so he wasn't much help to the police after his arrest in tracing Guru.

His interrogation revealed the existence of a HuJI-backed terror network in India, which was, in turn, getting support from the ISI.

Is Guru the sender of the first two emails? Is IM part of HuJI or just associated with it? Could we trace this Guru? I thought to myself.

Ravi replied, 'Sir, Amir Raza Khan is the younger brother of Asif Raza Khan, who with Aftab Ansari, had formed a terror network. Guru appears to be part of this group.'

Mohan added, 'Sir, the Guru who received explosives and the Guru who sent the emails, both could be one and the same person, as it can't be a coincidence that both had presence in Delhi, and both are terrorists. The police had an opportunity to try and apprehend Guru when Babu Bhai was arrested, but our laws are not flexible to allow us to keep the arrest hidden. As per D.K. Basu guidelines, we have to broadcast the arrests.'

The Supreme Court in D.K. Basu vs State of West Bengal (AIR 1997 SC 610) had laid down 11 specific guidelines that the police and other agencies have to follow for the arrest, detention and interrogation of any person. The purpose was to protect the rights of the arrestee and to ensure no one was kept in illegal custody. These guidelines, besides others, require that the arrest of a person should be made known to his/her relatives/known persons through various means. According to these guidelines:

First, the person arrested, detained or being interrogated has a right to have a relative, friend or well-wisher informed as soon as practicable, of the arrest and the place of detention or custody. Second, there should be a police control room in every District and State headquarters where information regarding the arrest and the place of custody of the person arrested must be sent by the arresting officer. This must be done within 12 hours of the arrest. The control room should prominently display the information on a notice board. Third, the person arrested has a right to meet a lawyer during the interrogation, although not for the whole time.

These guidelines serve to make the police force accountable to civil society and to ensure transparency in arrests being made by law enforcers. However, the one-size-fits-all nature of the law becomes a hindrance while dealing with terrorists and terror suspects. Suppose, a terrorist is arrested and the police has to pursue and arrest his associates as the next step. Naturally, when the broadcast is made of this arrest, the associate of the arrested suspect will go into hiding and vanish! If the information about the arrest of Babu Bhai could have been withheld from the ones known to him for a day or two, there was a very good possibility that Guru could have been apprehended and/or perhaps his whole network could have been unearthed in time, thereby saving many lives in subsequent blasts done by his group.

Ravi explained the similarities and differences between the bombs used in the recent explosions in Jaipur, Karnataka, Ahmedabad, Surat and Delhi.

Ravi summarized that the shapes of the explosive containers, except in Bangalore, were identical, i.e., a boat-shaped wooden

Place and Time	No. of Improvised Explosive Device (IED) exploded/ recovered	Timer	Power source	Explosive	Container	Detonator
Jaipur 13 May 2008	8/1	Quartz alarm clock with 1.5V pencil cell	9V Hi-watt make	Ammonium nitrate with embedded ball bearings	Boat-shaped wooden frame	Two electrical detonators in each IED
Bangalore 25 July 2008	8/1	Electronic timer circuit mounted on PCB of the size 4.5cm×3cm	9V power cell make	Ammonium nitrate mixed with binder	Cement concrete mould with embedded nuts and bolts	10 detonators, one electronic and nine non-electronic in each IED
Ahmedabad 26 July 2008	23/03	Quartz alarm clock with 1.5V pencil cell	9V Hi-watt make	Ammonium nitrate mixed with binder and embedded in ball bearings and nuts and bolts	Boat-shaped wooden frame	Two electrical detonators in each IED

Surat 27–30 July 2008 (recovery of unexploded bombs)	Nil/29	Electronic timer circuit mounted on PCB of the size 4.5cm×3cm	9V Hi-watt make	Ammonium nitrate with embedded ball bearings	Boat-shaped wooden frame	Two electrical detonators in each IED
Delhi 13 September 2008	5/3	Quartz alarm clock with 1.5V pencil cell	9V Hi-watt make	Ammonium nitrate with embedded ball bearings	Boat-shaped wooden frame	Two electrical detonators in each IED

frame with iron covering on the convex side. The container at Bangalore was made of cement concrete. Secondly, the timer devices at Delhi, Jaipur and Ahmedabad were identical and those at Bangalore and Surat were identical. Lastly, two electronic detonators were used at all the locations except at Bangalore, where 10 detonators—one electronic and nine non-electronic—were used.

The similarities between the bombs used in all the five cities made it evident that there was a common thread. The comparison further brought out that the bombs used in Delhi, Jaipur and Ahmedabad were identical and could be the handiwork of one group.

The timing devices used in Bangalore and Surat were identical. However, not even a single bomb exploded in Surat, while in Bangalore, out of nine bombs, eight had exploded.

'Can I have a look at the photographs of the timing devices used in Surat and Bangalore?' I asked.

Ravi showed me the photographs. The timing devices consisted of printed circuit boards (PCB) on which electronic items such as resistors, capacitors (electronic items that store electric charge), integrated circuit (IC) and diodes were mounted. Visual inspection showed that both the PCBs were identical, that means they were etched at one place or the same person designed the PCBs for both the places. Careful examination made it clear that in the case of timers used in Surat, one capacitor was missing, thus making it ineffective. This clearly indicated that the mounting of the electronic items for bombs in Surat and Bangalore were done by different people. Also, the container used in Bangalore was different from that used in the other four places.

'Ravi, the comparison of the bombs used indicates that there are three groups synchronously working together. One, probably located in North India, which caused explosions in Delhi, Jaipur and Ahmedabad; the second which attempted explosions in Surat and the third group which caused explosions in Bangalore, most likely located in South India. IM seems to be a big group spread over various parts of country.'

'IM had been using RDX before the arrest of Babu Bhai, and after his arrest, it started using ammonium nitrate as explosives. The arrest of Babu Bhai choked the supply of RDX to IM. This means that the Guru mentioned by Babu Bhai, and the Guru of the IM emails could be one person and he had received RDX from Babu Bhai. But unfortunately, Babu Bhai had no knowledge of the whereabouts of Guru. IM members were keeping their identity a secret, even from the people supplying logistic support to them. They were operating cautiously and discreetly.'

How can we find Guru? Who can possibly lead us to him?

4

THE BLINK OF AN EYE

16 September 2008
(The day continues...)

6.00 p.m.

I was working in my office when my intercom rang. It was ACP Rajan Bhagat, public relation officer (PRO) of the Delhi Police. He conveyed that portraits prepared through the key eyewitnesses—the 11-year-old balloon-seller in Connaught Place, Rahul, and the auto driver, Moolchand—were being released to the media and that he was sending copies to me and the Special Cell office.

My mind was preoccupied with thoughts on Guru, how to solve the blast cases and also apprehending the IM module. The success was dependent on various factors viz., the arrest of Subhan and Qayamuddin, dump data analysis result, response of the public on the portraits released, technical surveillance, analysis of CCTV footages and verifying purchasers of explosives.

◆

17 September 2008
(Two days before the Batla House shoot-out)

10.00 a.m.

Inspector Hridaya Bhushan and Inspector Lalit Mohan Negi, who had been working with the Special Cell for the past eight to nine years, came to my office. Both had an excellent track record and had received two police medals for gallantry work. They had also been rewarded by different state police for commendable work on several important terrorist and criminal cases.

During the course of our discussion, they threw up a name from the past that completely bewildered me. 'Sir, we have got feelers from Aftab Ansari, who has been sentenced to death in the American Center attack case in Kolkata of 2002. He wants to meet you in person in total privacy. He has information about the group responsible for these explosions.'

Now this was a name I was least expecting. *Aftab Ansari asking to meet me in private? Could he have credible information? Is Aftab's group still active? Amir Raza Khan was part of his group; does he want to give information about him?*

Aftab and I had crossed paths in July 1995. At that time, I was posted as DCP of the North-West District in Delhi. We had a case where a Delhi-based businessman was being threatened by a kidnapper named Dinesh Thakur, who was demanding ₹5 lakh as ransom. Ravi was tasked with apprehending Dinesh. As part of our plan, the businessman was asked to keep negotiating with the kidnapper and finally a deal was struck that he would pay ₹2 lakh to Dinesh in the Ashok Vihar market. A trap was laid by Ravi's team. When Dinesh showed up, the team tried to apprehend him, but he started firing at the police. The police also fired back in self-defense.

My office was very close to the market and upon hearing that the criminals have opened fire on the police party, I rushed to the crime scene. I saw that Dinesh was firing indiscriminately. The only way he could have been cornered was if someone engaged him from another direction. I started inching closer to Dinesh without him being aware of my position, but I was suddenly stopped by some shopkeepers. *What could that be? Why are they stopping me?* As I was trying to make sense of their behaviour, I noticed that they were trying to show me something, or rather, someone. I looked in the direction they were pointing at. I saw a man, Dinesh's accomplice who was trying to run away. Dinesh was busy with his shoot-out with the police and I decided to run after his accomplice. I started chasing him and after a couple of minutes, I saw a constable driving towards me. 'Sir, please get in the car. It will be easier for us to chase him,' shouted the constable.

Just as I was about to get in the car, the accomplice took a side road that was too narrow for the car to enter. I along with the constable gave him a chase and in a typical scene straight out of a Bollywood movie, the hide-and-seek started. He sneaked into by-lanes and gave us a tough time. But eventually, the proverbial long hand of the law got the better of him. On being confronted, he produced an identity that bemused us all. He said his name was Rajat Sharma and that he was a journalist. He claimed to be a common man. We frisked him and a firearm was recovered from this criminal-turned-journalist-turned common man. He was taken in for further interrogation.

Dinesh, too, was eventually overpowered by a volley of bullets from the police force. His accomplice turned out to be Aftab Ansari. Aftab was convicted in that case and after completing his jail term, he was released from the Tihar Jail.

This same Aftab later created a terror group with his associates. He executed the attack on the American Center on 22 January 2002 wherein four police constables and a private security guard were killed and 20 people were injured. He was arrested in Dubai on 23 January 2002 and brought back to India. He was convicted in this case and was sentenced to be hanged till death. Pending his hanging, he was lodged in the Kolkata Jail.

I immediately requested the IB to arrange for a personal meeting with Aftab at the earliest in the Kolkata Jail.

Meanwhile, we had a meeting with the CP. The Joint CP Ranges shared that many calls were being received from the public about people who matched the portraits of the terrorists, but none of them was found to have a suspicious background. They were following every information to its logical conclusion. They also briefed us that the verification of the people who purchased ammonium nitrate was at an advanced stage. The PCR had also requested other states to conduct the same exercise for people who had recently bought explosives. CCTV footages were being verified, but there was no credible information through this exercise yet. So, in short, there were no tangible results so far.

I reached my office shortly after this meeting. Alok, Sanjeev and Mohan visited my office to brief me about the suspected calls of Atif Ameen on 3, 6, 7 and 10 September. Atif's number had been taken into observation by our team sometime back. These calls were being reviewed to check if there were conversations that could lead us to the Delhi blasts. Mohan showed me the transcripts of the calls and also the voice recordings of the intercepts. We started analysing his call records and the transcripts.

First call on 3 September at 3.09 p.m.

A hawala operator called Atif addressing him as Ramesh. He conveyed to Atif that he (the hawala operator) had been tasked with delivering one and a half *peti* (₹1.5 lakh) to him and wanted to know where to deliver the amount. Atif enquired about the time of delivery and said that the amount should be paid in ₹500 bundles, and not in ₹50–100 bundles. Atif was talking as if he had been receiving hawala money in the past also. The hawala delivery person informed him that he could not confirm the time of delivery and denomination of notes, as he had not yet received the money. He asked the code number to verify if he was talking to the right person. Atif told him that delivery was to be made at Khalilulla Mosque, near the Batla House bus stand. The amount was received by Atif at 6.30 p.m. the same day. The second suspicious call was at 4.28 p.m. on 6 September between Atif and Mohd. Shakeel.

Shakeel (S): *Haan, bhaiyya.* (Yes, brother.)

Atif (A): *Kahan pahaunchey?* (Where have you reached?)

S: *Pahauncha hoon main ab wahan par.* (I have just reached that place.)

A: *Pahaunch gaye?* (Have you reached?)

S: *Haan...arre bhai yahan to bahaut pareshani hain...saamaan kaise lekar jaoonga main yahan se?* (Yes, brother, but there is great difficulty here. How will I carry the luggage from here?)

A: *Kyun?* (Why?)

S: *'Kyun' kya? Yahan to khade hone ki jagah nahi hain auto phauto ki.* (What do you mean 'why'? There is no place to park an auto here.)

There was another call between the two at 5.01 p.m.

Shakeel (S): *Haan, bhaiyya?* (Yes, brother.)

Atif (A): *Kya bol rahe the?* (What were you saying?)

S: *Haan, kuch nahi...mein ye keh raha tha ki, bhaiyya, wahan par to koi rukney ko raazi nahi ho raha.* (Yes, nothing. Brother, I was saying that no one is willing to stop or wait there.)

A: *Tab?* (What now?)

S: *Jagah hi nahi hoti hai.* (There is never any space.)

A: *Tab?* (What now?)

S: *Lekin ho jayega.* (But it will be done.)

A: *Ho jayega na?* (It will be done, right?)

S: *Haan, haan, wahi.* (Yes, yes, that.)

A: *Nahi toh tumhara murder likha hai aaj.* (Else, you are dead.)

S: (laughs)

A: *Mein tension mein so gaya tha.* (I had slept due to tension.)

During the above two conversations, the location of Atif was at Batla House while Shakeel's mobile location was at Karol Bagh. *Why were they so concerned about parking an auto?* The explosion at Karol Bagh had taken place in an auto. The call data records also showed that Atif had also visited Karol Bagh on 3 September. This conversation clubbed with the visit of Atif (his phone location) in Karol Bagh on 3 September created a suspicion about their involvement.

On 7 September 2.58 p.m., there was a call between Atif and someone he referred to as Hakim.

Hakim (H): Hello.

Atif (A): *Haan, Hakim, as-salamu alaykum.* (Hakim, peace be upon you.)

H: *Wa alaykumu as-salam.* (And unto you peace.)

A: *Atif bol raha hoon.* (This is Atif speaking.)

H: *Haan, maamu, bol.* (Yes, uncle, please tell me.)

A: *Kahan ho?* (Where are you?)

H: *Yahin Lucknow mein hoon.* (Here in Lucknow.)

A: *Lucknow mein ho?* (You are in Lucknow?)

H: *Haan.* (Yes.)

A: *Ek baat batao, khaali ho?* (Tell me one thing, are you free?)

H: *Haan, khaali hu, batao.* (Yes, I am free. Tell me.)

A: *Uske yahan Asad kuch saaman khareeda, tumhe maloom hain?* (There was some goods purchased at Asad's place, do you know about it?)

H: *Haan, haan, woh.* (Yes, yes, that.)

A: *Ab le ke aana hain. Wo Shadaab to aa nahi raha hain. Tumhe leke aana parega.* (Now, it is to be brought. Shadaab is not coming. You will have to bring it.)

H: *Haan to theek hain. Kab chaloon main, aaj ki kal?* (Okay. When do I start, today or tomorrow?)

A: *Haan, Asad se matlab batao ki mein lekar aa raha hoon. Bus se lekar aana hai.* (Yes, tell Asad that I am carrying it. Bring it by bus.)

H: *Haan, bus se.* (Yes, by bus.)

Another call was made between the two on 7 September 3.16 p.m.

Atif (A): Hello.

Hakim (H): *Haan, maamu.* (Yes, uncle.)

A: *Haan ji...* (Yes...)

H: *Hakim bol raha hoon.* (This is Hakim speaking.)

A: *Haan, Hakim, bol.* (Yes, Hakim, tell me.)

H: *8.30 baje ki train se aayen, ya bus se?* (Should I take the 8.30 train or the bus?)

A: *Volvo se.* (By Volvo.)
H: *Haan.* (Yes.)
A: *Aa jao.* (Come.)
H: *Haan, theek hain, main aa jaata hoon.* (Okay , I am coming.)
A: *Dekho, hisaab se leke aaye.* (Bring it with precaution.)
H: *Kya cheez?* (What?)
A: *Thoda hisaab se leke aana usko.* (Take precautions while bringing it.)
H: *Haan, mein samajhta hoon.* (Yes, I understand.)

It was clear from the above conversation that something was purchased in Lucknow and required to be brought to Delhi safely. Atif didn't want it to be brought by any other means except by bus. Why? Secondly, he wanted it to be brought very carefully. During the journey of the carrier from Lucknow to Delhi, Atif had made him numerous calls. Why? What was so important in that parcel?

We intercepted another call between Atif and Shakeel dated 10 September 2008 at 3.57 p.m. I am producing here the relevant portion of the conversation.

Shakeel (S): *Theek hain, sab badhiya...aur suno, mera bag le aaye ho?* (Everything is fine. Listen, have you brought my bag?)
Atif (A): *Arre yaar, abhi lekar aatey hain...ruko...abhi ja rahe hain...* (Friend, will bring it now...wait...I am going.)
S: *Hain?* (What?)
A: *Abhi jaakar lekey aa rahe hain na to tum hi kal aakar lelo apne hisaab se.* (I am going to bring it now, but you may get it tomorrow at your convenience.)
S: *Phir mein jummey wale din loonga na.* (Then I will take on Friday.)

A: *Phir kaise ganda karengey usko?* (Then how will we make it dirty?*)*
S: *Haan wahi to baat hain, isliye tum hi le lo.* (Yes, that is the problem, so you only take it.)
A: *Theek hai.* (Okay.)

What was meaning of 'how will we make it dirty?' Were they talking in code words? These calls were definitely creating suspicion.

6.00 p.m.

I reached our Lodhi Colony office. Sanjeev informed that dump data analysis did not yield any results. I asked him about interrogation of the SIMI activists. He told me that so far 15 SIMI members had been questioned, but it has not yielded any substantial results. The day was coming to an end and in spite of making some headway, it was a setback for us. Nothing seemed to be connecting or leading us closer to the perpetrators. But not trying was not an option. I always believed that even when there is darkness and success seems elusive, you should never lose hope and must keep trying, as you never know how close you are to success or light.

◆

18 September 2008
(One day before the Batla House shoot-out)

I left home at the break of dawn. While I was leaving, my wife Renuka asked me to come home early from office. I asked her why. She said, 'You forgot, today is Shruti's birthday.'

'Oh, sorry, I didn't realize today is the 18th! I will come home by 8.00 p.m.'

That morning at work went by analysing the information we had gathered so far. Sometime during the day, I received a call from the IB that the Kolkata Police was suspicious of Aftab's motives in demanding to meet alone and thus there was no confirmation regarding the meeting. They suspected that he might be trying to mislead the investigation. Even I had found this demand to be odd, but at this moment, we really needed more information, irrespective of who the source was. I asked the IB to try again. However, who would have known that a few hours from now we will be heading for our final operation.

Around noon, I got a call from Shri D.P. Sinha, joint director, IB, that changed the course of the day. He said he had some information coming from Gujarat and wanted to share it with me. Shri Sinha is an IPS officer (1977 batch) of the Manipur-Tripura cadre and had joined the IB in 1987. He has many years of experience in counterterrorism. I had worked with him closely in anti-terrorist operations since 1998.

I asked Alok to accompany me to the IB headquarters. Shri Sinha said, 'Karnal, you know that car bombs were planted in hospitals in the Gujarat blasts. These cars were stolen from Navi Mumbai. The Mumbai Police had arrested a car thief named Afzal Mutalib Usmani. He led the police to a house in Ahmedabad where he had seen a number of IM terrorists preparing bombs. He claims that he can identify them. He has also said that the module was led by a person named Abu Bashir, whose description he shared with us. It included the unique identification feature of protruding front teeth. This group of 13 members planted the bombs in Ahmedabad and thereafter, boarded the Rajdhani Express for New Delhi on 26 July 2008, just before the explosions took place. He further disclosed that Qayamuddin Kapadia, alias Rizwan, also travelled with the group.' Shri Sinha wanted us to act fast, as this was specific information. I promised him that the Delhi Police would take the lead very seriously.

This was a lead, but cracking it was a behemoth exercise. We had to track down each and every passenger travelling by Rajdhani on that particular day from Ahmedabad to Delhi. Starting at where they got reservation done could narrow down the search. *So, where should we start: Delhi or Gujarat?*

I shared this information with the rest of the team and asked them to obtain the list of passengers who boarded the Rajdhani Express from Ahmedabad to Delhi on 26 July. I also asked them to ascertain how many and who among them got the reservation done at any of the railway reservation centres in Delhi.

In the next two hours, Mohan and his team confirmed that reservation for 13 people was done from the Nizamuddin railway station. Unfortunately, the verification of the names and addresses given in the reservation foils did not lead to any results. It appeared that they had travelled with false names and addresses. I asked Mohan if the location of Atif's phone was at the Nizamuddin railway station at the time of reservation. After a few minutes, he called back confirming the same. *This could not be a coincidence.* My instincts were telling me that we were on the right track and that we have a lead to pursue.

'Mohan, we need to track the location of Atif's mobile phone, and all the numbers connected to him. Were any of these numbers present at the other blast sites before the Delhi blasts? Also, check their locations during the Jaipur and Ahmedabad blasts,' I said excitedly.

'I am on it, sir. You will have the results soon,' Mohan replied.

I knew I would have the results soon since I had put my best man on the job. Mohan's call tracking and human intelligence skills were unmatchable.

Just as I was trying to connect the dots in my mind, I got a call. It was my wife. 'By what time are you coming? Did you wish her?' I had completely forgotten. The day kept me away from wishing my daughter on her birthday!

'Give the phone to Shruti please?' I wished my daughter over the phone and promised her that I would be in time for the cake-cutting. She promised to wait for my return.

At around 7.00 p.m. at our Lodhi Colony office, we all got together to analyse the findings. Alok, Sanjeev and Mohan were present, too. Before the discussion, Alok said, 'Sir, today the police headquarters has issued orders for the transfer of all the five cases of bomb blasts (of 13 September) from the districts to the Special Cell. Which ACP should be assigned to these cases?[15] Do we allot all these cases to one ACP or distribute them?'

I thought over it and then looked at Sanjeev, 'I have tremendous trust in your investigative capabilities and the hard work you can put in. You should take up all these cases for investigation and collect the case files from the districts police.' Sanjeev was elated to accept the responsibility.

I asked Mohan to share the latest developments in the investigation. And as expected, Mohan was ready with his findings. He started by telling us that it was a strange coincidence that Atif's phone number showed no calls during the Jaipur, Gujarat and Delhi blasts. He showed us Atif's and his connected persons' call data records on the laptop. During the Jaipur blasts, there were no calls on Atif's number between 12 May (10.00 p.m.) and 14 May (1.00 p.m.). It could have been

---

[15]The case under UAPA is required to be investigated by the ACP and above.

switched off. Then before and during the Gujarat blasts, Atif's phone showed no calls during 11 July (1.07 p.m.) to 13 July (12.59 p.m.), 14 July (11.41 a.m.) to 17 July (1.45 p.m.) and 23 July (12.40 p.m.) to 27 July (10.01 a.m.)

During the Delhi blasts also, there were no calls on their numbers on 13 September (4.57 p.m. to 7.02 p.m.). Even the numbers that Atif was in touch with showed no activity during the Jaipur, Gujarat or Delhi blasts.

Mohan added that we had already discussed about the suspicious intercepted calls of Atif and the presence of his and his associates' numbers at the bomb sites in Delhi prior to 13 September.

'What about its location when the emails were sent by IM from Shakarpur and Sahibabad?' I asked Mohan.

'The email on 23 November 2007 (during the blasts in the UP courts) was sent from Shakarpur, East Delhi at 1.18 p.m. During that time, this phone showed no calls from 12.17 p.m. to 2.57 p.m. Similarly, the email from Sahibabad was sent on 14 May 2008 at 8.44 p.m. Even then, there were no calls at this number from 7.12 p.m. to 9.16 p.m.' Mohan said with the surety of someone who had done his research well.

Besides, the phone number 9714552899, which was one of the three phone numbers confirmed to be used by terrorists in the Gujarat blasts, was in Delhi on 17 July 2008 and returned to Ahmedabad on 23 July. Atif's phone was also active during this period in Delhi and was having no calls prior or after these days. The location of the number 9714552899 when it was in Delhi, was also in Jamia Nagar. Who was carrying this number? The above analyses clubbed with the strange intercepted calls on Atif's number were casting strong suspicion on Atif.

I looked at Mohan with a deep sense of appreciation, 'The three numbers used by the terrorists in Gujarat were with the Gujarat Police, central intelligence agencies and the police of other states. But only you and your team could identify Atif's number as suspicious. You are a genius and an asset to the organization. Keep it up! We need a watertight plan to apprehend Atif. He will have information on the other members. He should not slip away from our hands. He is the key and our only hope right now of cracking this case.'

Mohan said that he was sending a team to get familiarized with the area—Batla House locality in Jamia Nagar—and also his teams would try to apprehend Atif if he moved out.

'Good, once you have the plan, let us review it and get the teams ready.'

Mohan immediately directed a team led by Ravinder Tyagi to do a surveillance of the area. While enroute, Ravinder was given additional input from the team intercepting calls that Atif had a plan to meet his brother, Ragib, at Abul Fazal Enclave in Jamia Nagar. Therefore, they were asked to keep a close watch at both the locations. The team was asked to intercept and bring Atif in if there was any movement.

Suddenly, my cell phone rang. It was my wife calling. 'You are still in office?' she sounded concerned.

'Listen, Renuka, I'm sorry, but I will not be able to come for the party. Please carry on and I will make it up for this later,' I was apologetic.

'It's okay. We understand. You take care,' she said and I could see her smiling on the other side.

The silent sacrifices that a cop's family endures on a daily basis!

While awaiting the outcome of the surveillance done by Ravinder's team, I rang up the CP and Shri Sinha at around 9.30 p.m. and shared with them the latest developments on the case. Shri Sinha came to our office within an hour and I took him through the investigation in detail and all the evidences that we were able to collect thus far. He was pleasantly surprised that we were able to get on a lead in such a short time.

In the meanwhile, Mohan got a call from Ravinder that there was no activity at either of the places and, therefore, it was decided to close the surveillance operation. Now, we had to decide on the next plan of action. We felt the team needed to act without any delay in apprehending Atif, as that would help conclude if he was really involved in terrorism. The team was unanimous in its decision to raid Atif's location—L-18, Batla House.

The crucial question was, when?

It was the month of Ramadan and, hence, it was not advisable to search in the evening or night. Mohan suggested that we should search Batla House during daytime since this is the time when they would be resting at home.

A plan was initiated and two teams were formed. 'Mohan, you lead the first team. Make sure that you are discreet during your search operation and if we do not find anything, no one should have an inkling of our presence in that area. Sanjeev, you will be heading the back-up team.'

I had a general discussion with the officers. Before heading home, I visited the interception room once and talked to the officers there, from whom I came to know that Mohan's son was suffering from dengue since the past few days.

While leaving, I spoke to Mohan. 'How is your son now? You didn't tell me that he is unwell.'

'Sir, he has been hospitalized. Doctors say he is now out of danger. He has been given blood transfusion. I am heading there now.'

'Why didn't you share this with me before? You should be with him in such a time.'

'Don't worry, sir, my wife and my parents are with him. I have been talking to them regularly. I did not say anything before as this case is very important. We cannot lose more lives.'

'Mohan, I am really proud of you! I wish your son a speedy recovery. Please let me know if any help is required.'

'Yes, sir, good night.'

Little did I know then that that was the last time I would be seeing Mohan.

5

THE ADDRESS THE NATION WILL NEVER FORGET

19 September 2008
(The day of the Batla House encounter)

I was sitting alone in Sanjeev's office at Lodhi Colony. My teams were already enroute to Batla House. This was the first lead in many days that had the potential to bring more information on the blasts.

It was also a very hectic and important day for the Delhi Police as Union Home Minister Shri Shivraj Patil was visiting its headquarters to interact with all the officers of the rank of DCP and above. I was expected to be present at the headquarters. However, I knew I had to be available to my teams at all times during critical operations, so I decided to stay behind. While briefing the CP that morning about the status of the investigation and the raid to be conducted, I had sought permission that Alok and I be exempted from attending the meeting with the Home Minister.

When people go for such operations, they prepare themselves for all possible scenarios, but sometimes, unexpected turn of events demand instant decision-making. People leading the war against terrorism are aware that they may not always know everything, as the enemy is hidden and there are still pieces of the puzzle missing. Although we had a strong suspicion about Atif, we were not totally sure about his involvement in the crimes.

Two teams had been sent for this task. Mohan led the first team consisting of 18 police personnel including himself. The police were in casual clothes so as not to attract unnecessary attention. This team was backed by another smaller team led by Sanjeev. The second team was supposed to act only if some unexpected situation emerged.

The past few days had been difficult for everyone as most of them had hardly been home and were working round the clock. After leaving from office at 2.00 a.m. the previous night, Mohan had gone to check on his son in the hospital. His son's platelet count was dipping, but he was assured by the doctors that he would recover. Satisfied, he then bid his family goodbye and told them that he would be seeing them in the evening. Mohan had handpicked his team. They had a long association and were partners in many anti-terrorism operations and fight against dreaded gangs. It was a big day for him, too, as he was very instrumental in tying up the loose knots of the leads.

Rahul had just returned to Delhi after an operation in Pathankot. He had been so busy the past few days that his daily routine of morning walks and then dropping his son off to school was disturbed. While he was leaving for office, his wife said, 'Don't forget that tomorrow morning we have to go for an interview with the principal of DPS for our son's admission.' He assured his wife he would be there and left for office.

Ravinder had reached home very late on the night of 18 September. His wife served him dinner and asked the reason for the delay. He told her that he, along with team members, were busy in an important operation related to the recent blasts. He left for office early the next day.

Dharmender was called back from Srinagar, where he was working on a terror-related operation. He got a call from the office asking him to be dressed as a Vodafone Cellular Company representative. He was used to such disguises for the purpose of collecting information. He reached home in the wee hours and hastily got ready to report at office. He said goodbye to his parents and wife. He told them that they were hoping to crack the blast cases soon and asked them to pray for his team. He also had a fleeting glimpse of his two kids, who were fast asleep. On his way out, he shared a light moment with his mother—like on any other day. He reached office and from there, he drove to Batla House with Mohan.

HC Balwant Singh was a frontrunner of the team in numerous operations. Bullets could never deter him. On 18 September, he was returning from J&K with a team of the Special Cell. They were pursuing a JeM module there. He was hoping to catch a train from Ambala to his village in UP. As he was about to board the train, he got a call from the Special Cell office asking him to reach early the next morning, as a raid was to be conducted. He changed his plan and reached office at around 5.00 a.m. He briefly spoke to his wife over the phone and told her that he would come home after the raid.

HC Udaibir Singh lived in a rented accommodation in Vasant Vihar, New Delhi, with his school-going son, while his wife and daughter were back in their village in Hapur, UP. He was working on an operation in J&K and had asked his son to eat at their neighbour's house during his absence. By the time he reached Delhi on 18 September, it was already quite late. He did not want to disturb his son and stayed overnight with his colleague in Burari instead. From there, he went straight to his office in the morning and joined the raid party.

HC Satender Singh was the concerned father of a teenage daughter and son. He used to be worried about their studies and also carried the guilt that he was not able to give them enough time. On 18 September, he, along with other team members, returned from J&K. When he reached home late at night, everyone was asleep. Without speaking to anyone, he left early for office the next morning.

SI Rakesh Malik had hardly visited his home after the blast. He was responsible for intercepting the calls and as such was very busy in the control room.

SI Devender Singh returned from J&K on the night of 18 September, had a quick meal, took a nap and left for office very early the next morning.

Assistant SI (ASI) Anil Tyagi started his day early. He got ready in a kurta-pyjama, bid his wife goodbye and left for office.

HC Satender Kumar was to take his 19-day-old baby boy and his wife for a routine check-up. He missed his doctor's appointment that day, much to the disappointment of his wife. He left for office very early that day.

HC Vinod Gautam was confined to his office since 13 September, as he was assigned multiple tasks in the ongoing investigation.

Constable Birender Negi also couldn't go home after 13 September because of the ongoing work. He had a quiet birthday with his colleagues on 17 September in the office itself.

HC Manish Kumar skipped his bath, got ready in a kurta-pyjama and casual slippers. His wife asked him why he was leaving so early, to which he replied that there was some important work at office. He hugged her and left the house.

Constable Sandeep Singh was part of the team that was investigating a kidnapping case in Keshav Puram when he was asked to report for the blast investigation. He visited all the blast sites to ascertain the cell IDs of those locations required to obtain the mobile towers' dump data from all the service providers. He was able to go back home only once since 13 September. On 18 September, he was in the Batla House locality, doing a recce and familiarizing himself with the area. He remained in the area till 2.00 a.m. and returned to office in the wee hours.

SI Dalip Kumar was in the office with Mohan till late night on 18 September. He got up early that morning, took a bath, went to the temple and offered panchamrit on the Shiva Linga and left for office on his two-wheeler. He wanted to speak with his kids before leaving, but couldn't.

Constable Rajeev was posted in the Special Cell since 2006. He also had to come back from J&K with the team. He had a spare key of his house. When he reached home, he quietly opened the door without disturbing his wife and daughter. He took a bath and caught up on some sleep before leaving for office early the next morning.

HC Rajbir Singh was a wrestler and his colleagues called him 'Pahlwan'. A soft-spoken and courageous man, he, too, had returned from an operation in J&K a day before. When he reached home, he milked his buffalo, skipped his breakfast and reported on time for the Batla House operation.

Sanjeev, who was leading the back-up team, had been so immersed in his work during that week that he and his wife were having constant arguments over his unavailability. That morning also they had an argument. As he was about to leave for the operation, she requested him to drop her in Vasant Vihar. While he was on his way, Mohan updated him about the team's position at Batla House. He dropped his wife on the roadside and rushed to the spot! This despite the fact that they just had an argument in the morning.

They all had familial responsibilities, emotionally strained spouses (rightly so), and children or/and older parents to be taken care of, among other things, but when it came to the call of duty, everything was secondary.

This was my team. And we were ready for the Batla House operation.

I was in constant touch with my men. The raid could start any moment. Just then, a call came in. It was from Mohan. 'Sir, there are people inside L-18. We are going in.' I wished him luck. It was around 11.00 a.m. then. I was getting anxious to know the outcome of the raid and was waiting for the next call from Mohan. Every second felt like hours.

After about 10 minutes, my phone rang. This time it was Sanjeev. 'Sir, Mohan and HC Balwant have been shot and are being shifted to the hospital. The terrorists are also injured, but they are inside the house.' His voice was choking, as if he was in tears. I had never seen Sanjeev like this.

I was shocked, but I controlled myself. 'Sanjeev, are Mohan and Balwant okay? How bad is their condition?'

Sanjeev only repeated himself, though this time he was in better control of his emotions. We both were silent for a few seconds and the silence said it all. We knew that our colleagues were injured, that this was the most unfortunate part of any operation, but the operation had to continue. I gathered my thoughts and instructed Sanjeev to try to contain the terrorists. They had to be taken in alive to extract information about their network. I told him that I would reach there as fast as possible and that I was also requisitioning for additional force. I immediately collected the remaining officers present in the Special Cell and left for the venue. Simultaneously, I sent a message to Alok to meet me on the way.

Oh god! Hope Mohan and Balwant are okay.

I called the CP, but he did not pick up the phone. I realized that he must have been in the meeting with the Home Minister. I asked the PCR to immediately dispatch five companies of force and one platoon of commandoes at L-18, Batla House.

In a few minutes, Shri Neeraj Kumar, special commissioner of police, rang me. 'Karnal, what happened?' He was my predecessor heading the Special Cell and was second-in-command in the Delhi Police. 'Sir, Mohan's team conducted a raid at L-18, Batla house. There was an exchange of fire in which Inspector Mohan and HC Balwant have sustained bullet injuries. I have requisitioned more force and I am going to the spot.' He told me that the force was being sent and DCP South, Dhaliwal, who was present at the Delhi Police headquarters, had been asked to reach there, too.

Alok met me on the way and we both reached Khalilullah Mosque near Batla House by car and moved on foot to L-18. The situation there was tense. A huge crowd had gathered near the mosque, shouting slogans against the Delhi Police. The crowd looked agitated and it seemed that any moment, they could charge on us. I looked around and found that additional force had still not reached. I still had to go to L-18, the scene of the encounter. As we passed the mosque on the left, we took a right turn into a long street of around 130 meters. L-18 was halfway into the street. This walk was one of the most tense moments of my career. I could sense animosity for the Delhi Police in the by-lanes. A few vehicles were parked on the street and a number of locals were standing and whispering to each other. After walking some distance in the street, we entered L-18 on the left and climbed to the fourth floor, where we met our team. Flat no. 108 was on the left side from the stairs. Sanjeev was standing there with his team. He told me that they were able to enter the flat and that there was a brief encounter. One person had been detained.

The flat had two entry doors perpendicular to each other. The stairs led to the front gate and on its left was the second door. We entered the flat using the side door, which opened in a small lobby. To the left was a toilet and in the front were two rooms, one on the left and one on the right, with a kitchen in between. As I turned right after entering the lobby, there was a living room. I noticed bullet marks on the walls and empty cartridges and bullet leads strewn all over the floor. There was blood on the floor. A person was lying on the floor injured, or could have been dead too, in the living room and another was in the left room. One pistol each was seen near them. One AK-47 was also recovered later. I took a closer look at the person lying in the living room. *He could be Abu Bashir as his description matched the one we received from the Gujarat Police.* I asked Sanjeev to send their photographs to the IB immediately and to get it verified by the Gujarat Police. Simultaneously, both of them were immediately shifted to a hospital.

Then, I asked my team to explain the sequence of events. Rahul explained that Mohan was leading the front team. All the team members, except Dharmender, were asked by Mohan to be in casual wear. This was done to ensure even if the target was not found in the apartment, the team could withdraw without anyone knowing about their presence or the search. That was also the reason why none of the team members were wearing bullet-proof jackets. The team had met at Abbasi Chowk, where a final briefing was given by Mohan. On Mohan's instructions, Rakesh and Manish were sent by Rahul to Shaheen Bagh for some verification. The vehicles were parked near the Khalilullah Mosque on the main road. The team had carried bullet-proof vests and AK-47 weapons, but had left them in the vehicles in the custody of Birender, Sandeep and Satender Singh (in case needed in any follow-up operation). They carried only small arms with them. The team walked towards L-18, Batla House. On their way in, the Khalilullah Mosque was to their left. The team then took a right turn into a street. Dalip and Anil were deployed on this street. HCs Vinod and Rajbir were deployed on the left side street towards the mosque, while SI Devender and Constable Rajiv were on the right side street. They had been asked to keep moving around so as not to cause any suspicion about their presence. L-18 was almost in the middle of this long street, to the left. A seven-member team then entered the building that had a parking area and one flat on the ground floor. A few vehicles were parked there. A staircase led to the remaining four floors of the building. Each floor had two flats, one on either side of the stairs.

While Mohan and five officers waited at the bottom of the staircase, Dharmender was sent to the fourth floor to confirm if there was any activity inside Flat no. 108. Sporting a white shirt and dark-coloured trousers, with a shoulder bag, Dharmender was disguised as a Vodafone executive (Atif Ameen was using a Vodafone SIM card).

He went up alone to the gate of Flat no. 108 and heard the sound of people talking inside. He came down and informed Mohan, who, in turn, informed someone on the phone. Then, the seven-member team comprising Mohan, Dharmender, Ravinder, Rahul, Balwant, Udaibir and Satender Kumar (two officers in the 18-member team had the same name) reached the door of Flat no. 108. Mohan was in front and he tried to push open the front door gently. The door was closed from inside. The team then knocked at the door, disclosing their true identity. Suddenly, there was silence inside the flat. The team made some effort to open the front door, but were not successful. The raiding party then observed that the side door was unbolted and it could be opened.[16] As soon as Mohan and his team entered the flat and found themselves in the lobby, they were greeted by a volley of shots fired at them from the living room and the room on the left. The team had landed in the crossfire and responded instantly in self-defense by firing back. Satender and Udaibir immediately entered the room on the right. Ravinder took shelter near the kitchen, from where he fired at the assailants, while four officers (Mohan, Rahul, Dharmender and Balwant) remained face to face with the three assailants in the living room. The terrorists were trying to escape by opening the front door while constantly firing at the team. In the ensuing battle, two suspects managed to escape and one fell down near the front door. Mohan and Balwant sustained bullet injuries. By then firing had stopped from the left room. Dharmender and Udaibir took Mohan out of the building and from there, they, along with Devender and Anil, took Mohan to the Holy Family Hospital at Okhla Road. Ravinder took Balwant downstairs and handed him over to HC Gurmeet Singh, who took him to the AIIMS Trauma Centre.

During this period, only two officers, Rahul and Satender, remained inside Flat no. 108. They covered the left room, where some assailants were hiding. Ravinder came back upstairs and he and Satender covered this room, while Rahul came out to check the two assailants who had escaped from the flat. He could barely check the roof and Flat no. 107 when the back-

---

[16]Later, Zeeshan, the co-accused who used to stay in the flat, revealed during interrogation that he had left in the early morning for his exams while others were still asleep. He exited the house through the left gate and, therefore, it was not found bolted from inside.

up team headed by Sanjeev reached the fourth floor and took stock of the situation. Sanjeev's team was in bullet-proof gear.

Sanjeev narrated that as soon as he reached Jamia Nagar, he received a call from Dalip, a member of the raiding team, who informed him that Mohan had been shot at. Within no time, Sanjeev reached the spot. By this time, the three constables who were in the vehicles with AK-47s and bullet-proof vests also reached the gate of L-18. Dalip, who was positioned outside the building, led Sanjeev upstairs to the flat. Rahul updated him of the situation. One of the terrorists was lying injured in the living room, whereas, some were still hiding in the other room. When the team tried to enter the left room, the terrorists started firing. One of the assailants moved from the left side of the room towards the balcony door. As the police fired at him, he fell on the floor. When the team tried again to enter the room, he started firing at them all the while trying to get up. Sanjeev and his team fired back. Rajbir, who had accompanied Sanjeev, did a burst fire with his AK-47 that neutralized him. Rajbir was shot at twice, but was saved thanks to his bullet-proof vest. One of the terrorists, Mohamad Saif, was found hiding inside the toilet of the left room and he surrendered himself. He disclosed that the person lying injured in the room was Sajid and the one lying near the door was Atif Ameen. He, at that time, did not disclose the names of the two people who had escaped. An AK-47 assault rifle and two loaded magazines with 30 rounds each were found in the room on the right, beneath the mattress. Both the injured terrorists had used .30 pistols.

Days of working to find the lead, planning, strategizing—all came to an end within a few minutes. Flat no. 108, L-18, Batla House was now an address the entire country knew.

◆

Acutely aware of the fact that this encounter might take its own life in different political circles and that it will be flashed in the media with ample amount of conjecturing and speculations, the first thing I needed to confirm was the veracity of the events as it unfolded. I enquired in detail about the positions of the officers and inmates during the encounter. Their version was in consonance with the bullet marks and other spots in the flat. I inspected the whole house while the teams searched and collected the evidence such as laptops, cell phones, documents, weapons, etc. I also went to the roof and the adjoining flat.

The tension in and around Batla House area was mounting. At this time, Dhaliwal also reached the flat. He told me that the additional force had arrived. I asked him to make law and order arrangements in the area as while coming, I had observed that some people were trying to instigate the crowd. 'And yes, the district police should immediately take over the investigation of the encounter,' I asked Dhaliwal to get this done on priority. The National Human Rights Commission's (NHRC) Guidelines stipulates that any encounter should be investigated by the police unit other than the unit involved in the encounter. So, the investigation of the encounter was handed over to the district police immediately and subsequently the task of investigating the encounter was transferred to the Crime Branch of the Delhi Police.

I came down to the street that was by now swarming with mediapersons with their cameras and OB vans. I could see a huge gathering of locals, angry and raising slogans against the Delhi Police. I had to address the impatient media and give them the initial information to quell speculations and hearsays. I remember talking to them briefly and then excusing myself.

My mind was at Holy Family Hospital, where Mohan was fighting for his life. Anxious faces of our officers greeted me at the hospital. Mohan's condition was not stable, nor was he in a position to be shifted to AIIMS. The doctors were doing their best and we could only pray. Specialist doctors from Apollo were also called in. Soon, I saw his wife and other family members coming towards us. It was a difficult moment for all of us, to look into the eyes of the family members, not knowing what to say. Words of consolation and encouragement sound so hollow. Spending some time with his wife and family however eased the pressure off me as well. We were all in this together and collectively praying for his recovery. We were one big family.

◆

However, despite the grave situation, the investigation had to go on. We still needed to find out who these people and their associates were and their involvement in the blasts, if any. We also had to know if Atif was actually Abu Bashir. I talked to team members and asked some of them to stay there and others to take up further investigation. I spoke separately with Dharmender, who was in the leading team with Mohan and inquired about the incident. He corroborated the sequence as was told by Rahul. We then went to the AIIMS Trauma Centre to check on Balwant. Upon reaching, I asked about his well-being and about the incident. His version was identical to those of Rahul and Dharmender. I was almost convinced that we were on the right track and that the encounter was genuine.

While I was on my way to the Delhi Police headquarters, I got a call from Rajan, the PRO of Delhi Police. He sounded worried. A TV channel was flashing the breaking news that the terrorists had been hiding in the Khalillulah Mosque. Naturally this news was creating panic and apprehension in the residents of that area, who feared that the police would enter the mosque. 'Is this true? Could you please confirm, sir?' asked Rajan. 'This is absolutely wrong information! There are no terrorists in the mosque and neither does the Delhi Police have any intention of entering the holy place,' I responded. The news was immediately contradicted by the PRO, thereby controlling the unpleasant situation that could have arisen due to this false and irresponsible reporting.

By the time I reached the police headquarters, news arrived from the IB that testified our investigation. Atif Ameen was indeed Abu Bashir and that Mohamad Saif and Sajid were involved in Ahmedabad blasts.

How spot on was Mohan!

We now had to organize a press conference immediately to counter all the rumour and misinformation, which unfortunately was travelling fast and wide.

The CP briefed the media in detail:

As you all are aware that there were blasts in Delhi on 13 September. The Special Cell of the Delhi Police immediately swung into the investigation of these blasts. We remained in constant communication with the Gujarat Police, Rajasthan Police and the central intelligence agencies. The Special Cell had been developing intelligence to identify the terrorists who were behind these blasts. We got information that one of the key suspects of not only the Delhi blasts but of others as well was hiding in Batla House. A team led by Inspector Mohan Chand Sharma and backed by another team led by ACP Sanjeev Yadav reached at around 11.00 a.m. at Batla House. During the operation, the terrorists opened fire on the police team, which retaliated in self-defense. At least eight bullets were

*fired by the terrorists while the police team fired 22 rounds.
Inspector Mohan Chand Sharma, who was leading the
team sustained bullet injuries. His condition is critical. I
would like to say that Inspector Mohan Chand Sharma is
one of the most decorated officers in the country. He is the
recipient of one President's Police Medal for Gallantry and
one police medal for gallantry and five bars. That means
he has received seven gallantry medals. He is critical and
we are very hopeful that he will come out of this. All our
prayers are with him. Another officer of the Special Cell,
HC Balwant Singh, has also got a bullet injury on his hand.
He has got a fracture there. I had visited both the officers.
HC Balwant is being operated on and steel plate will be
implanted. In the operation, Atif, alias Bashir, who was the
main leader of the IM, and one Sajid were killed. Both of
them are residents of Azamgarh and presently were staying
in the Batla House area. It is found that Atif is linked with
the blasts all over the country. The signature of the bombs
defused in Delhi on 13 September consisting of wooden
frame and use of two detonators and type of timer device,
were seen in the bombs used in Jaipur, Ahmedabad and
Hyderabad. We also have information that he, along with
other associates, left for Ahmedabad from Delhi on 23
July and returned to Delhi on 27 July. He was present in
Jaipur also when the bomb blasts took place in Jaipur. We
are developing further information in this regard. I would
also like to clarify that at this moment, Abdul Bashar, who
was involved in the Gujarat blasts and brought to Delhi on
remand by the Gujarat Police, has got nothing to do with
this operation of the Special Cell today. Some of the news
channels are running the story that Abdul Bashar was
brought from Gujarat and he pointed out some houses on*

the basis of which this operation was carried out. I would like to categorically state that that information is totally incorrect. This information was developed by the Special Cell. We have recovered one AK-47 with ammunition and two regular imported .30 pistols besides computers and other material which are being examined further.

On being asked as to who all have been arrested, the CP replied, 'We have arrested one person while two were able to escape.' The media further asked if Abdul Subhan Qureshi, alias Tauqeer, was one of the persons who escaped. The CP replied that the investigation was on to ascertain the identity of the escapees. He also told that Mohamad Saif was caught from the spot and he was being interrogated and that the team was investigating the case further. 'Everything happened too fast and details will be obtained with further investigation. We are at the moment concerned about Inspector Mohan Chand Sharma and HC Balwant and we are following up on their medical condition closely. We are also following investigation and as we have more information, we will revert to you.' He stated that Tauqeer had links in the Delhi blasts and was the key man pushing the operations.

One of the journalists asked, 'Raids are conducted generally at 3.00 a.m.—when everyone is sleeping, why was this raid conducted during the daytime?'

The CP was aghast at this question, 'I don't know your motivation of asking a question of this nature. There is no fixed time to catch a thief. No one says, "Please come to arrest me between 1.00 a.m. to 4.00 a.m." The police had information, so went there at 11.00 a.m. to arrest him. What is wrong in that?'

He also confirmed that the Delhi Police had also got inputs from the Gujarat Police.

Once the press conference was over, I, along with Alok, excused ourselves and rushed to Holy Family Hospital to enquire about Mohan. It was around 7.00 in the evening and a large number of well-wishers had assembled there. Somehow I was feeling a bit uneasy and felt something was wrong. We walked through the crowd and reached the intensive care unit (ICU) where Mohan was kept. Inspector Sanjay Dutt took me to a separate room. Soon, the doctors came out and their expression said everything. Mohan could not be saved now. He was breathing his last. We rushed to his room and saw him lying connected to machines and wires that were trying to save him. I walked towards him, put my palm over his forehead and tears started flowing from my eyes. The very life of the Special Cell, the man whose investigation yielded us results, the one who could beat any encrypted message and intercept any call, the one whose network of human intelligence was immaculate, was lying there connected to machines and wires. The man who would make a difficult task easier by his words, 'Ho jayega, sir...ho jayega (It will be done, sir. It will be done)' was lying there, lifeless. I knew that we had lost him.

In extreme grief, I went to another room. I called Mohan's father and informed him. He was in total shock and was inconsolable. At that time, the Union Home Minister along with the CP also reached the hospital.

No words can fill the gap that his absence left in his family's lives. I felt lifeless, devoid of any thoughts or emotions. No one could have imagined that our day would end like this.

When life-changing events occur, we do not get any signs that they are about to happen. You live on as if each day will be routine. And these moments creep in, when we least expect them and they change our world forever—a world without a brave, soft-spoken and committed comrade like Mohan.

6

DRAMA IN THE STUDIO

This is an extremely painful moment for all of us and for Mohan's family. We lost a brave and brilliant officer today. It was his excellent investigative skills and efforts which brought the Delhi Police great success—great success, but great and unbearable pain, too. He had led the team in unravelling the mystery of the Indian Mujahideen (IM), the outfit responsible for the explosions and the killing of many people, month after month. He went ahead in this mission even though his son was struggling with dengue in the hospital. For him, his duty was supreme and more important than anything else. He always worked in mission mode and accomplished solving the most difficult cases. His soul is now looking at us to see if we can accomplish his unfinished task. I know we all are filled with deep sorrow and grief at this juncture and in no mood to work on. But by doing so, we will be failing Mohan and the people. If he were here, he would have asked everyone to follow the leads without losing any time. And we must do that! We owe it to the people of this country and to Mohan, the sacrifice that he has made. We must honour it by continuing his legacy of cracking difficult cases.

Prarabhyate nakhalu vighnabhayen Neechaih,
Prarabhya vighnavihata vismaranti madhyah
Vighneh punah puarapi pratihanyamaanaa, Prarabhya
chottamajanaa na parityajanti

(The fear of obstacles stops the inferior men from starting work. Medium men start their work, but leave it midway whenever they face difficulty. Exceptionally good people start their work, and continue with it even if there is a series of obstacles in their way.)

—26th Sholka, Nitiśatakam of Bhratrihari

You are the best people who can't be stopped by any difficulty, any sorrow or any pain. Let's put in our best. We need to work fast so as to catch the leads and move on. Let us meet in the Lodhi Colony office in an hour to regroup and work on the next steps and as Mohan would have said: 'Let's follow the lead'.

I said these words trying to hold back my tears.

◆

Mohan's team did not want to leave the hospital as they wanted to be there for his family. They were filled with a sense of deep sorrow at having lost an old associate, a colleague and a mentor who they had worked with on many cases. Empathy flowed in for Mohan's family: his young wife, his children, one of whom was fighting dengue in the hospital, his daughter, parents who have just lost their young son, and his sisters.

There was pain all around. The pain of losing a dear and daring colleague, the pain of seeing his grieving family, the pain that the culprits were still at large and needed to be apprehended. We had to get back to our duty and move fast to unearth the mystery of IM.

We were all in this together, as a family. I had full trust in Mohan and my team. I asked a few of our officers to stay back in the hospital with Mohan's family and asked the others to reach our Lodhi Colony office, where a crucial task lay ahead of us: that of questioning Mohamad Saif, who was found hiding in the toilet at Batla House during the encounter.

I walked into the room and saw Saif sitting on a chair. A young man of medium height, he had a wheatish complexion and curly black hair. He was looking down at the floor. Sanjeev was able to get some information from him, albeit with some initial hiccups. Inside the ordinary-looking young man was a tough and radicalized mind and I have often wondered how much poison can be filled in a person to make him a changed man! On sustained questioning, he started revealing things in parts and narrated how he became a part of IM. He also elaborated on his role in various terrorist activities in the country. The son of a PCO owner, Saif was born in 1987 in Sanjarpur village, in the Azamgarh district of UP. His father, Sadab Ahmad, apart from running a PCO near a taxi stand in Sarai Mir, a town and a nagar panchayat in the Azamgarh district, was actively involved in politics. He was in fact the district office president of the Samajwadi Party. Saif was in class eight when he started listening to lectures organized by SIMI on several topics including jihad. It is here that seeds of radicalism and extremism were planted in him.

Saif carried on with his studies and completed his B.A. degree from Shibli National College, Azamgarh, in 2006. Thereafter, he took admission in an M.A. course in Pandit Govind Ballabh Pant Mahavidyalaya in UP. His elder brother, Dr Shahnawaz Alam, was already friends with Atif Ameen and Sadique Israr, alias Sadakat (one of the leaders of IM, he had motivated Atif to join IM), and the two of them often visited the brothers. They were the ones who motivated Saif to join their group. Saif also came to know that his elder brother had already undergone training in Pakistan.

We were in the middle of questioning Saif, when suddenly I received a call from a news channel. It informed me that a young man named Zeeshan was in their office claiming he was afraid that he would be arrested by the Delhi Police for the blasts. Zeeshan claimed innocence and wanted the media house to protect him. The channel informed us that they would be conducting his interview and if he was wanted by the Special Cell, I may send a team to their office to arrest him.

Why is the media house asking us to arrest or detain this person from their studio? Is this a ploy to get more mileage from the ordeal? I responded that the media should carry on with the interview and inform me once the interview was done. Naturally, the channel was expecting some drama to unfold in their office what with the Special Cell zooming into a newsroom and nabbing the culprit. Alas, I played a spoilsport in this media frenzy!

'Who is this Zeeshan?' I asked Saif. He did know Zeeshan and confirmed his role in the Ahmedabad blast. I mobilized a team headed by Rahul to be stationed near the news channel's office where Zeeshan was taking refuge, albeit a temporary one.

After some time, another call came in from the same channel that they would hand over Zeeshan to the police and that I could send my team to their studio in Paharganj. No way was I sending my men to the news channel.

'You may please decide what you want to do with Zeeshan. Our Special Cell officers will not enter your premises,' I responded as a matter of fact. So, left with no other option, the channel let Zeeshan go. Our officers detained him as he was leaving the studio.

Meanwhile, the same channel was repeatedly calling and asking if the Special Cell had arrested Zeeshan. I replied saying that the decision regarding his arrest would be taken only after we had confirmation that he was indeed involved in the blast cases. Soon after, the IB confirmed Zeeshan's involvement in the Ahmedabad blasts.

During the course of Saif's interrogation, more revelations were made. Saif was one of the first ones to join Atif's group and he took part in all the explosions caused by the group. He gave vivid descriptions of the bombs planted by this group on 23 November 2007 in the UP courts in Faizabad, Lucknow and Varanasi, 13 May 2008 in Jaipur, 26 July 2008 in Ahmedabad and 13 September 2008 in Delhi. He also revealed the role played by different group members in every blast. Saif narrated how Atif radicalized his schoolmates, his friends and the friends of his friends. Atif was the one who knew the source of explosives used in the cases. He was aware that the Surat module of IM had brought the explosives for Gujarat blasts. He disclosed that he along with Mohamad Khalid had brought the materials from Manipal from someone named Shahrukh for the Delhi blasts.

Zeeshan was the next to be questioned. He was about the same height as Saif and had a small build. He kept a black moustache and his hair was short and flat. Initially, he feigned ignorance and declared that he didn't know anything.

'Zeeshan, we are sending your photograph to the Gujarat Police to verify your involvement in the explosions there. So, it is best to be honest with us and tell us your story,' I told him curtly.

Meanwhile, we sent his photograph to the IB to confirm whether he had a role to play in the explosions in Gujarat and other cities. After some time, we received affirmation of his involvement. Breaking under interrogation, Zeeshan had no choice but to reveal the truth.

Twenty-four-year-old Zeeshan Ahmad belonged to Azamgarh, where his father was a lecturer in a government inter-college. After completing his schooling from Azamgarh, the city lights beckoned him. He came to Delhi in 2002 and took admission in B.Com in Zakir Husain College. In 2005, he got admission in the Indian Institute of Planning and Management (IIPM) and, two years later, landed a job in Monarch International, an export house in Kalkaji. He then took a rented flat in C-4, Janta Flats, Okhla Vihar, in May 2008. Zeeshan now had a job and was living away from his parents. His evenings were spent with his distant maternal uncle, Atif and Atif's friends who lived near Zeeshan. The group frequently met and discussed atrocities on Muslims and also about jihad. Atif's laptop, which we recovered later, had a PowerPoint presentation titled 'Inhuman Gujarat', in which the Muslim community was shown to be targeted. The visuals and descriptions of the post Godhra riots of 2002 were effectively employed to mould young impressionable minds. It was particularly Mirza Shadab Beg, an associate of Atif, who succeeded in radicalizing him.

After numerous such sessions, one day Zeeshan took one and half day's leave and went with his group to Ahmedabad by the Ashram Express. It was 11 July 2008. Atif had instructed everyone not to use their real name and they were given fake Hindu names.

The next morning, all of them got down at the Ahmedabad railway station. In Ahmedabad, Atif divided them into groups and each group did the recce of distinct locations for planting the bombs. Most of them returned to Delhi by the Ashram Express the same day, except Saif, Chhota Sajid and Bada Sajid, who stayed back in Ahmedabad. Shadab (another of their accomplice) told Zeeshan that they had planned to carry out blasts in Ahmedabad tentatively on 19 July, for which all the planning was done. However, on 15 July, Shadab told him that the consignment of explosives had been delayed and they had to postpone their plan from 19 July to 26 July. Zeeshan took a half-day leave for 25 July and a full-day leave for 26 July from his work. On 25 July, they left again for Ahmedabad by the Ashram Express. Atif and Chhota Sajid received them at the Ahmedabad railway station and took them to a two-storied house in a densely populated area. He went in and saw that many bombs wrapped in different colour tapes were kept on the floor of the first floor of the house. A cloth banner was tied on the wall which read 'La Ilaha Illalah Mohammad Rasullah: Indian Mujahideen (There is no other god than Allah, and Mohammad is Allah's prophet: Indian Mujahideen).'

At about 3.15 p.m., the teams dispersed to plant the bombs. Immediately thereafter, they assembled at the railway station. All 13 of them along with one Rizwan, alias Qyamuddin, came to Delhi by the Rajdhani Express.

In August 2008, Atif and others shifted from Janta Flats to L-18, Batla House, which was taken on rent by Atif. It is in this house that they made their plan to carry out blasts in Delhi. Zeeshan then gave details about the Delhi blasts and how they recced the various locations and who planted the bomb at which locations.

After planting the bombs in Delhi on 13 September, they returned to L-18, Batla House and saw the news on the TV about serial blasts in Delhi. They congratulated each other on their success. Confident about their success in Delhi, the group now had plans to target the financial hub of the country, Mumbai.

On 19 September, the day of the Batla House encounter,

Zeeshan had gone to take an exam, while the others were still sleeping in the flat. He had quietly opened the side door to leave the house, without disturbing others. When his exam was over, he saw the news of the police encounter at L-18, Batla House. At first, he decided to leave Delhi but nervousness got the best of him. He called a few of his friends and his mother, who advised him to take the media route. And this was how he had approached this particular news channel.

The interrogation continued till late that night. I left the office at about 2.00 a.m. after deliberating on the work to be done during the day.

7

PICKING UP THE PIECES

20 September 2008

I reached home at around 3.00 a.m. and before I could get any sleep, it was already time to leave for office. It had been a week since the blasts and a day since the encounter at Batla House. There were still many leads to be followed, and that required extra hours at office.

9.30 a.m.

As per the protocol laid down by the NHRC, when a death happens during an encounter, the concerned department needs to send an initial report on the incident to the NHRC. These provisions have been in place since 1997 and were revised in 2003. There is a specified format for the report and it should be sent to the NHRC within 48 hours of the incident. The second report is to be submitted within three months of the incident. The encounter is also investigated by an independent agency, preferably by the Crime Branch of the state, which on completion of the investigation, submits its report to the judicial magistrate, where judicial scrutiny of the encounter takes place. As per the NHRC guideline, the government should also institute a magisterial enquiry.

These provisions are in place as checks and balances to ensure police officers are accountable for their actions on the ground.

I prepared the first report to be submitted to the NHRC detailing the incident. I was reading the final proof of the report when I got a call from Sanjeev. 'Good morning, sir, the post-mortem of Mohan's body has been conducted at AIIMS and the body will be shifted to his residence shortly.' 'Okay, Sanjeev, please keep me posted,' I replied and hung up. A few officers of the Special Cell and South District were present with Mohan's family at the hospital to support them during this harrowing time.

I reviewed the report, dispatched it to the NHRC office and called the CP to update him regarding the outcome of the interrogation done the night before. The time and the location (Nigambodh Ghat) of Mohan's cremation were also shared with him. He asked the Joint CP, Northern Range, to make security arrangements at the cremation ground, as a large number of people were expected to be there.

While in office, I flipped though the newspapers that had extensively covered the Batla House encounter. One national daily read: 'Delhi Police mourns its Braveheart.' All the newspapers covered the exemplary work done by Mohan. One of Mohan's relatives had shared that:

At a time when most fathers would have stayed beside their sick son's hospital bed to tend to his blood transfusion and ensure that dengue died down, Inspector Mohan Chand Sharma rushed to Jamia Nagar from the hospital to raid a house where terrorists were holed up. Sharma had not gone home for three straight days, rushing from office to hospital and back. His wife expected him to finally return on Friday evening. But home they brought the warrior dead.[17]

Mohan was one of the top officers in the Delhi Police known for fighting against terror. He was exceptionally gifted in technological understanding and had great command over surveillance and in tracking down criminals. I was also quoted in the article: "'We have lost our best man,' lamented Joint Commissioner (Special Cell) Karnal Singh, his boss.'

My mind drifted to the operations carried out by Mohan's team. Mohan was an excellent leader with many years of experience of working on the ground. I felt pangs of pain as I read the newspapers. It still felt like he would walk into my office any moment with his cheerful smile. I wished it was all a nightmare and things would be different when I woke up. *But this is the reality.* I brought myself to read the other news stories. A few of the snippets focused on SIMI. One news item read:

> *Investigating agencies say the shootout has bared the real character of the Students Islamic Movement of India as consisting of fanatics who have no compunction in massacring innocents, possess deadly bomb-making skills and have a cache of sophisticated weapons... This comes at a time when the Centre is building a strong case in the Supreme Court for reversing the order of the Unlawful Activities (Prevention) Tribunal lifting the ban on SIMI. The tribunal turned down the Centre's plea to extend the ban, saying the Home Ministry had failed to back up its*

---

[17]TNN, 'Nation Mourns Gallant Cop M.C. Sharma,' *The Times of India,* 20 September 2008. Available at: https://timesofindia.indiatimes.com/city/ delhi/Nation-mourns-gallant-cop-M-C-Sharma/articleshow/3504200.cms. Last accessed on 2 July 2020.

*case with evidence. The Centre retorted that the tribunal
had not taken up the volume of evidence put before it.*[18]

The Government of India had banned SIMI for the first time on
26 September 2001 under the Unlawful Activities (Prevention)
Act 1967. The ban continued for two years and then it was
again imposed on 26 September 2003. The ban was imposed
for the third time on 8 February 2006. On 5 August 2008,
the special tribunal of the Delhi High Court lifted the ban
giving the reason that, 'Material given by the Home Ministry
is insufficient, so ban cannot be continued.' The government
immediately moved the Supreme Court, which stayed the order
of the tribunal on 6 August 2008. The present investigation
had brought out a plethora of evidences against the activities
of SIMI, thereby strengthening the case of the government
against SIMI which could be presented in the Supreme Court.

Another news item read:

*The death of an inspector in Friday's encounter will also
make it difficult for powerful politicians in the Government
to argue for lifting the ban on SIMI. Two members of the
Manmohan Singh Cabinet—Railway Minister Lalu Prasad
and Steel Minister Ramvilas Paswan—had hailed the
tribunal order against the ban as a validation of their belief
in the 'innocence' of the organization. They were joined by
the UPA's new-found ally, Mulayam Singh Yadav, who as
the chief minister of UP, refused to enforce the ban on SIMI
in the state.*[19]

---

[18]'Mask Torn Off SIMI's Hardline Face,' *The Times of India*, 20 September 2008.
Available at: https://www.pressreader.com/india/the-times-of-india-new-delhi-ed
ition/20080919/281535106798135. Last accessed on 13 June 2020.
[19]TNN, 'Delhi Encounter Exposes SIMI's Real Face,' *The Times of India*,
20 September 2008. Available at: https://timesofindia.indiatimes.com/Delhi-
encounter-exposes-SIMIs-real-face/articleshow/3505181.cms. Last accessed on

The political undertones in some of the articles did worry me about the potentiality of a political fallout of the encounter due to the divided opinions in the ruling coalition. There were news articles that highlighted the community efforts to maintain peace and calm.

This community radio run by the AJK Mass Communication Research Centre of Jamia Millia Islamia university appealed to people to maintain calm and restraint. Immediately after the news broke about the encounter, the radio station that was playing recorded programmes and was about to shut for Friday namaz, came alive with its volunteers taking stock of ground zero and going live on air. Its anchor Arfa, a PhD scholar in political science, announced,

> *From time to time, these anti-social forces try to create disruption in our society. We need to be united and fight these forces. What happened here today is not related to any religion or creed. We want to tell you that this issue is between the police and anti-social elements. Dear listener, you should stay indoors at this hour. Don't believe in rumours, there is no danger to you.*[20]

I admired the selfless and timely contribution made by the students in dispelling the fear in the minds of the people and coming out openly against terrorism.

After the post-mortem, Mohan's body was carried to his residence at Dwarka. A large number of neighbours and people from far-off places had gathered in the locality.

---

13 June 2020.
[20]Manash Pratim Gohain, 'Radio Jamia Plea Helped Maintain Calm in Area', *The Times of India*, 20 September 2008. Available at: https://timesofindia. indiatimes.com/city/delhi/Radio-Jamia-Plea-helped-maintain-calm-in-area/ articleshow/3504986.cms. Last accessed on 13 June 2020.

Many of them did not know him personally, but they felt the highest regard for him and had come there to pay their last tributes. Sanjeev informed me that the procession was starting from Mohan's home. I left my office with Shri Dadwal and reached the cremation ghat, where the local police had made arrangements for the last rites. Slowly, the gathering grew to an unprecedented level and it included the common men as well as the who's who of Lutyens Delhi. Home Minister Shri Shivraj Patil, Delhi Chief Minister Mrs Sheila Dikshit, BJP leader Shri L.K. Advani, Lieutenant Governor (LG) Shri Tejendra Khanna and police officers of every rank and cadre, advocates and hundreds of citizens came to pay their respects. Mohan was a national hero.

Mohan's body was brought to the cremation ground in a van that was decorated with flowers. When his body was taken out from the van, Shri Dadwal and I moved forward to give shoulders to carry him to the base floor, where wreaths were laid on his feet. The police's armed contingent gave *salami* (salute) with a volley of bullets to the departed soul. Thereafter, his body was carried to the pyre at Yamuna bank. Everyone present was tearful and filled with immense grief. His family was inconsolable.

Shri Gopal Subramanium, Additional Solicitor General of India, was standing beside me. He had met the officers of the Special Cell during numerous legal briefings. He knew Mohan very closely and was quite fond of him. He spoke to me and expressed his solidarity in fighting against terrorism. I remained there till the cremation proceedings were over. On my way back to office, I spoke to Alok and Sanjeev.

'Sir, I think we should now tell the public what we know so far about the the IM module,' Alok was convinced of this.

Delhi Police Commissioner Shri Y.S. Dadwal, Joint Commissioner Karnal Singh and other officials carrying the body of Inspector Mohan Chand Sharma for his last rites.
Image credit: PTI

'Okay, Alok. This makes sense. The people should know the details of the terror networks,' I concurred with him.

I asked Rajan to call for a press conference. My phone rang again, it was from DCP South, Dhaliwal. 'Sir, the owner of Flat no. 108, L-18, Batla House came to the police station with a police verification form. It had an acknowledgement stamp of the police station on it. The form was given to him by the caretaker of the house as proof of police verification.'

'Oh, it means there was a lapse on our part?' I quipped.

'No, sir. On enquiry, it was found that the police station stamp on the verification form was forged and no such form was ever submitted in the police station. It was also found that the caretaker forged the signature of the owner on the tenancy deed,' Dhaliwal said.

'Good work! Do follow every lead that comes your way,' I replied.

It was time for the press conference. As I entered the PCR, the media was waiting with bated breath. Not an inch of space was left unoccupied. Television cameras with their wires extending to their OB vans were ready to beam live pictures, the mikes positioned like an artillery. The energy of palpable. I went live.

Yesterday morning, an encounter took place at Batla House in which we lost Inspector Mohan Chand Sharma, one of our best officers. He has worked with me for the last four and a half years. He was very energetic and worked indefatigably. His analytical abilities and field performance were unparalleled. Mohan Chand Sharma's team, supervised by ACP Sanjeev Yadav and DCP Alok Kumar, was able to pinpoint the exact location of this module of IM within a short span of time. Thereafter, he conducted a search in order to apprehend the inmates of the Flat no. 108, L-18, Batla House. Unfortunately, there was an exchange of fire with the inmates in which Inspector Mohan Sharma sustained bullet injuries, while HC Balwant got bullet injury fracturing his hand. Mohan succumbed to his injuries last evening. He is survived by his wife and school-going son and daughter. I pray for his family. Our team was emotionally disturbed after the demise of Mohan Chand Sharma, yet the team was working continuously without any rest. Last night, the team worked till 2.00 a.m. Mohan's and his team's efforts bore fruits. One Mohamad Saif was caught from Batla House and Zeeshan was caught yesterday night. Interrogation revealed that Atif was the main person behind IM. However, within a short span of time since their arrest, at least it is established that IM is supported by SIMI and HuJI. They are backed by the LeT.

The intelligence inputs during last three–four years have revealed that Pakistan's ISI has changed its strategy and decided to use Indian residents in terrorist activities so that ISI can deny its role internationally in such heinous activities in India. Funding was done by the LeT, while the logistic support was provided by SIMI/HuJI. We have come to know about the perpetrators of the Delhi blasts. Atif and Junaid planted bombs in Greater Kailash. Sajid, who died during the encounter, and Zeeshan planted the bomb at Barakhamba Road. Interestingly, the portrait that we got made from the inputs of Rahul, a balloon-seller, matches with Zeeshan. Shahzad and Shadab planted the bombs at the children's park, Mohamad Saif and Khalid planted them at Regal Cinema, Mohamad Shakeel planted the bomb at Gaffar market, Senior Sajid (other than who died in the encounter) and Zia-ur-Rehman planted the bomb in Central Park, Connaught Place. They had recced the places on 11 September. The explosives used in the Delhi blasts were brought from Karnataka, and the evidences are being collected to explore routes in Karnataka. The laptop seized from the spot is being analysed. It contains evidences of emails sent by IM and material related to terrorist activities. It also contains a logo-designing software, using which they appeared to have designed the IM's logo. However, the complete forensic report is still awaited. All the persons involved in the Delhi blasts hail from Azamgarh. Atif radicalized his classmates, seniors and juniors and motivated them to join terror activities. Nine of them had gone to Jaipur on 11 May 2008 and recced the town to identify hotspots for explosions. They returned to Delhi on the same day. Again, on 13 May, they took a morning bus from Delhi to Jaipur, purchased cycles, planted bombs in them and returned to Delhi. We have recovered the mobile that was used to make the video clip of the cycle with a bomb placed in Jaipur. The same clip was sent along with the email by IM on 14 May 2008. On 11 July, 11 of them went to Ahmedabad by train. Three of them stayed back to manufacture the bombs, while the others returned to Delhi. On 26th the group reached Ahmedabad again to execute the blasts. They had got local support there who assisted in planting the bombs. Later some of their local accomplices were caught by the Gujarat Police.

This group is also responsible for blasts caused in the courts in 2007 in UP. We have identified 13 members of this module by now and information has been shared with other states including UP and intelligence agencies. We will cooperate with all of them so that this (entire) module is caught. Intelligence sharing is very important. IB, the Gujarat Police and the Rajasthan Police shared sufficient intelligence with the Special Cell. The sharing helps in nabbing the terrorists by various police agencies, as the state police can work based on intelligence obtained from other agencies/state police. We must all unite in the war against terrorism. We have to work meticulously in tracing the evidence and identifying and arresting other members of the IM module. We have to trace the origin of the explosives; we have also got leads about the funding.

After I was done addressing the media, a volley of questions was thrown at me.

Q: Sir, there are reports that a 14-year-old boy was also part of this module?

A: This information is floating on the basis of interrogation in Gujarat wherein a 14-year-old boy was mentioned as being part of the module. It was Sajid, who died in encounter. The information about his age is incorrect and investigation has established that he was not minor.

Q: What was the motive of this group in killing people? Was it to terrorize them?

A: We have found enough material in Atif's computer to indicate that he was baptized by the philosophy of the Al-Qaeda. A good amount of material relating to the Al-Qaeda has been recovered including the photographs of Osama Bin Laden. He was inspired by him. By the way, photograph of Subhan (wanted in the Gujarat blasts) was also found in his laptop.

Q: Could IM be considered a dead horse now?

A: I will not say that. Two have died and two have been caught. We have to arrest many of them. Besides, the Surat group is yet to be uncovered.

Q: How is Abu Bashar (who was caught from UP by the Gujarat Police) linked with IM?

A: The interrogation of Abu Bashar made it amply clear that he has allegiance to SIMI. The Nagori group of SIMI had decided to take recourse to terror path and organized training camps for its members. SIMI approached IM through Tauqeer (Subhan), who talked to Bhatkal, and then Atif. Abu Bashar has told during the interrogation that they had got communication with IM and has also given details about that. Therefore, two groups, SIMI and IM, have been working together. They formed a deadly combination and had the support of the LeT.

Q: *What is the profile of Atif?*
A: Atif was 24 years old. He was taking some course on human rights. He used to travel to different places in India. He had contacts all over the country. He used to speak less. He did not allow his group members to carry mobile phones with them during planting of bombs. A mobile was carried to Jaipur for making a video clip of the cycle with the bomb, but this mobile was devoid of any SIM card.

Q: *Was there tenant verification done by the landlord?*
A: There is one Mohsin Nisar, who is an executive engineer working in UP. This house is owned by him. His steno is Abdul Rehman. They (Atif and his associates) approached Abdul Rehman through his son. They told Mohsin that a Jamia professor and two students want to hire the house. No verification form was received in the Jamia Nagar police station. They also prepared a lease deed on 25 August, that is also forged.

Q: *There was police station stamp on the verification form?*
A: The stamp on the verification form was also forged. Since you talked about the stamp, let me tell you something more. They travelled to Gujarat via a train under assumed names, one such name was Rahul Sharma. When we asked Saif if he had gone to Gujarat, he denied it. We recovered a voter card in the name of Rahul Sharma having his (Mohamad Saif's) photograph. It was forged and had a stamp of the Election Commission. He was asked why he got this forged identity card. He purchased the SIM card on the basis of forged documents and after huge bill accrues, he would throw the SIM card and never pay the bill. They had prepared forged identities for travel, etc. They were made on the computer.

Q: Does the Delhi module have any connection with the Surat bombs?

A: Not the Surat bombs, but yes, Ahmedabad, Jaipur and Delhi bombs were the handiwork of the Delhi module. We are still tracking the Surat module.

Q: How did they escape?[21]

A: There were two doors in the house. While the encounter was on, they managed to escape through the front door while firing at the police. There was an initial melee and confusion that helped them escape.

Q: What is the role of Tauqeer (Subhan) and Abu Bashar?

A: Both are from SIMI. They had organized training camps and gave lectures on jihad. Their role is very important. SIMI has been planning for important individual targets and general targets.

Q: What are the names of the 13 persons belonging to the Delhi module?

A: Atif alias Bashar, who died in the encounter; Mohamad Sajid alias Pankaj, who also died in yesterday's encounter, Shahjad alias Pappu; Junaid (Pappu and Junaid had escaped from the encounter place), Shadab Bhai alias Malik; Sajid (Bada Sajid); Mohamad Khalid, Arif, Zeeshan Ahmad, Shakeel, Zia Khan (Zia-ur-Rehman), Salman. The name of 13th person is not yet known.

Q: Why was Zeeshan arrested?

A: When Zeeshan was brought to the Special Cell office, he claimed that though he was staying with them, he was not aware of their activities. We told him if he was not involved, he would be allowed to go. We told him that his photograph will

---

[21]Two people had escaped from L-18, Batla House during the encounter.

be sent to Gujarat to verify whether he was involved or not. After some time, he said that he wanted to say something. Then he told us about his role at two places, Ahmedabad and Delhi.

Q: How many state police were working on the blast cases?
A: Every state police is working very hard. The IB is coordinating with them and each and every piece of information has been worked upon meticulously. To begin with, terror-related intelligence is not specific. It is very difficult to develop that indistinct intelligence input and requires tremendous work. This information developed by Mohan Chand Sharma was not precise to begin with. Developing the information, ascertaining that the leads developed are in the right direction, i.e., whether they are terror related or not, and then further following the leads and developing field intelligence is a long and tedious process. It is not like catching a criminal. The officers who have worked in anti-terror units understand how much labour and efforts are required in this area.

Q: Why was the National Security Guard (NSG) team sent to the spot?
A: The NSG team was sent because I got information from Sanjeev that Mohan has received bullet injuries and terrorists are still holed up in the flat. I asked the police headquarters to send five companies of force and one platoon of commandoes immediately, as we didn't know at that time what steps might be required to handle the terrorists. Do we surround the area or take some other steps? One has to think of such eventualities in advance and, hence, the NSG team was asked for.

Q: Why were bullet-proof jackets not used?
A: Inspector Mohan Chand Sharma was no novice, as he had faced many difficult situations and led many operations

including the operations in Kashmir. He was an expert and perfectly knew what steps were to be taken. Not wearing of bullet-proof jacket was part of his strategy to merge with the surroundings without being detected. If one goes for verification wearing bullet-proof jacket, the person could be identified from a distance and the operation can fail. According to him, it was a perfect plan. Knowing fully well that he was leading a team to catch a terrorist and that too without putting on a bullet-proof jacket, Mohan knew it could be fatal, yet he went there risking his life. Only a person who has a deep desire and ambition to serve his country would have the courage to take such a tough decision. We must appreciate his bravado.

The press conference was over and terms such as Batla House, the Indian Mujahideen and modules became a part of household discussions.

◆

21 September 2008

The next morning, most newspapers carried the details of the investigation conducted by the Delhi Police and about Mohan's last rites. One national newspaper stated:

...Delhi bid a tearful adieu to its hero on Saturday. People from all walks of life joined Inspector Mohan Chand Sharma, who laid down his life fighting terrorists on Friday in the Jamia Nagar encounter, in his last journey... His body, wrapped in a white cloth with a Delhi Police flag on him, reached his home in south west Delhi's Dwarka around 1 p.m. on Saturday afternoon in a vehicle decorated with flowers. It was accompanied by his colleagues from the Special Cell and family members. 'We have not only lost

*a fine officer, but also a beloved friend and a great leader,'
said one of the members of the team.*

*Onlookers outside his building, who had been waiting
since morning for Sharma's mortal remains to arrive,
shouted slogans like 'Mohan Sharma Amar Rahe, Bharat
Mata Ki Jai (Long live Mohan Sharma, Long live India)'
and queued up to pay their last respects when his body was
laid down. 'We didn't know him personally, but we came
when we heard that his body would be brought home. He
was a very brave man and a hero to all of us. Maybe not
directly, but in more ways than one, he saved the lives of so
many people by shooting down two terrorists and busting
their cell. We need more officers like him to fight terrorism
in this country,' said an onlooker.*

*But, Sharma, the martyr, was the only son of his
parents, Damodar and Devindri Sharma. 'He may be a
hero to the world, but he was my only son. Heroes can be
replaced by others, but who can replace a son, a father, a
husband and a brother?' asked his mother. Sharma's wife,
Maya, his daughter, Himani and son, Divyanshu, who was
discharged from the hospital on Saturday morning after
being treated for dengue, were inconsolable.*[22]

Another news read:

*Wreaths of marigold and rajnigandha. An unusually
tearful police force. And crowds chanting 'Jab tak suraj
chand raheja, Sharmaji ka naam rahega.' A distraught city
turned up for the funeral of its very own braveheart ...The*

---

[22]Medha Chaturvedi, 'Thousands Bid Adieu to Friday's Shootout Hero,' *The Times
of India*, 21 September 2008. Available at: https://timesofindia.indiatimes.com/
city/delhi/Thousands-bid-adieu-to-fridays-shootout-hero/articleshow/3508053.
cms. Last accessed on 13 June 2020.

*cremation at Nigambodh Ghat was conducted with full
police honors and attended by the home minister.*[23]

Another news item gave a totally different perspective about
Mohan:

*Also an ordinary man with ordinary fears. Gangotri said
her brother had a morbid fear of elevators. He may have
eliminated 36 hardened terrorists and 40 inter-state
gangsters, arrested 80 militants and 129 gangsters and had
been one of the most promising officers of the Delhi Police,
but Inspector Mohan Chand Sharma was still an ordinary
man.*

*According to Gangotri, Sharma's elder sister, he was
afraid of elevators and used to feel claustrophobic while
using them. 'He was very brave, but when it came to using
elevators, he had a morbid fear. He would always prefer
stairs, though he lived on the seventh floor. He didn't mind
climbing all those flights of stairs rather than risk being
stuck in an elevator,' she recalled. 'When he and his wife,
Maya, bought this apartment, he once got stuck in the
elevator. He made such a fuss about it that he almost sold
off the flat.'*

*She added he was very energetic. 'He would work
throughout the day, and yet when he returned, he was full
of energy. He used to make it a point to spend some time
with his children every day, however late it may be,' she said,
unable to hold back her tears. According to her, Maya and
Mohan were a very loving couple who never fought. 'The*

---

[23]Radhika Oberoi and Rahul Tripathi, 'Tearful Farewell for Fallen Police Hero,'
The Times of India, 21 September 2020. Available at: https://www.pressreader.
com/india/the-times-of-india-new-delhi-edition/20080921/281535106798635.
Last accessed on 13 June 2020.

*first major fight they had was on Friday morning when
Maya asked him to stay back and take care of their son,
Divyanshu, 13, who was admitted in the hospital, suffering
from dengue. His platelet count had gone down to 20,000.
Committed to his job, he fought with her and left for the
encounter, promising to return early,' she said. ...Sharma's
mother, Devindri, said, 'He was too committed to his work,
was almost a workaholic. When it came to his work, he never
listened to any of us. He had such a beautiful life. He was my
only son and had five sisters and two young children whom
he looked after very well. He has left a void in our lives.*[24]

I could not hold back my tears. I was in deep thoughts about
the pain Mohan's family would be going through. I recalled that
Mohan, along with four other inspectors of the Special Cell,
had visited my residence at around 8.00 p.m. on 12 September.
They told me that the police headquarters had moved a file
for their transfer from the Special Cell. As they were in the
midst of following up on a few critical modules, they should
not be transferred. I asked them where the transfer file was,
to which they replied that it was in the office of Shri Neeraj
Kumar, Special CP Administration. I immediately spoke to
Shri Kumar over the phone. He declined receiving any such file.

As I was remembering that day, my chain of thoughts
was broken by a call. DCP Dhaliwal was on line. 'When your
live press conference was on air yesterday. Bhisham Singh,
ACP, who was enquiring into the issue of forging of tenant
verification form was also viewing it. When he heard the name
of Zia-ur-Rehman as a member of the IM team, he immediately

[24]Medha Chaturvedi, 'Also an Ordinary Man with Ordinary Fears,' *The Times of India*, 21 September, 2008. Available at: https://www.pressreader.com/india/the-times-of-india-new-delhi-edition/20080921/281603826275371. Last accessed on 13 June 2020.

suspected that Zia could be the son of Abdul Rehman, the caretaker of Flat no. 108, L-18, Batla House. This lead led to further raids and arrest by the team of Inspector Brijender Singh (working under ACP Bhisham Singh) of Mohamad Shakeel, Zia-ur-Rehman and Saquib Nissar. On interrogating them, they confessed to be a part of the IM and to causing explosions,' Dhaliwal sounded jubilant.

'Excellent! Work further on the leads obtained from them. Compliment Bhisham Singh and his team on my behalf for this excellent work.' Elated and proud of Delhi Police teams, I immediately informed the CP and Shri Sinha of the latest development in the case.

Since this case was unfolding in the public eye, every detail was scrutinized and examined. It is often said, it is false information that always reaches first and, hence, the challenge was to curb this fake dissemination of news. After discussing with Sanjeev, Alok and other team members, it was decided that we will share the relevant information with the media without impacting the investigation.

Another press conference was called and I started the briefing:

Further interrogation of Mohamad Saif has provided more revelations. They (this group) are also found to be involved in the blasts that took place at Sankat Mochan temple in Varanasi in 2006...and Gorakhpur in 2007... We have found some interesting clips and photographs in the Atif's laptop. In one photograph (photograph shown to press) Saif is sitting and there is a caption 'Most wanted'; similarly a photograph of Sajid (who died in the encounter) also has a caption 'Most wanted'. The copy of the memory stick from Atif's phone was analysed in the cyber lab. It has video

clippings and photographs of the bombs placed together
making the shape of IM and on the back of it, a piece of
cloth is hanging on which it is written 'Indian Mujahideen
Ahmedabad'. These bombs were subsequently planted and
exploded in Ahmedabad. We have recovered more clips
relating to the Gujarat blasts. That is a very good piece of
evidence that links them with the Gujarat blasts.

After the address, the floor was open to questions by the
press.

Q: Sir, the Home Minister of Karnataka has given a byte that
no explosive for the Delhi blast was obtained from Karnataka.
A: I will not comment on the byte given by anyone. We are
working on the basis of evidence collected during the course of
our investigation. We have already tied up with the Karnataka
Police. We are aware where Mohamad Saif stayed in Karnataka
to procure the explosive. He gave graphic details about it.

Q: Who was giving instructions to Atif?
A: Till now, we have not reached any conclusion about the
person who used to give instructions to Atif. The investigation
so far has revealed that he was one of the topmost in the
hierarchy of IM. The team has been working on the various
modules of IM and soon we will know more about them.

Q: Have you got the examination report of the bombs used in
Delhi?
A: Formal examination report has yet not been received.

Q: Educated minds are taking part in terror activities. What
should be done about it?
A: Social education is required to be imparted to individuals
and this, unfortunately, is beyond the scope of police work.

Q: It is said that the IM group doesn't send emails to each other, but is saved as draft. The other person opens the same email and reads the draft, as a result the documents on their mails do not travel and, therefore, it is not possible to detect?
A: Let me clarify that your proposition that these people do not send the mail but save as draft and so it doesn't move on the network is not scientifically correct. Whenever you save the mail, it is uploaded and saved on the mail server and, therefore, there is communication between your computer to the server through the service providers. When you read the saved email, it gets downloaded from the server to your computer. However, some people have got a misconception that if the email is saved, it doesn't travel on the network.

Q: They had been operating from Sarai Mir for a long time, is it not the failure of local intelligence?
A: Actually, they were working at various places—Delhi, Mumbai, etc., and they had taken up different jobs or had taken admissions in colleges. These people never talked about their terror activities or about their views, so one never really knew about their plans and activities. Therefore, to say that it was a failure of certain intelligence units is not right. It is the most difficult job to collect intelligence or conduct investigations in terrorism-related cases.

Q: Could you tell us the support that SIMI has provided to this group?
A: They have provided support structure and manpower. The Gujarat Police have already arrested some of them. The interrogation of those arrested by the Gujarat Police provided clues that led to ultimately solving the mystery of IM.

Q: Was Tauqeer the mastermind of the Delhi blasts?

A: Atif was the main man in the planning and execution of the blasts in Delhi. However, Tauqeer on the SIMI side and Atif on the IM side were coordinating terror activities between them.

Q: By when will the other IM terrorists be caught?
A: Many Delhi Police teams and of the other states have been working to apprehend the remaining terrorists and we are hopeful that they will be caught very soon.

Q: The Gujarat Police had said that SIMI and IM are one, while you are saying that they are different?
A: The information is not static. This was said by the Gujarat Police a month ago and since then, a lot of information has come up in several directions. It will take some time for the whole mystery to unearth and we are working towards it.

The press conference ended on a note that was conciliatory. The media was satisfied with our response and we were transparent about our findings and leads. However, a surprise awaited me the next morning. I received a call from the CP conveying that the Home Ministry did not want us to indulge in any more media briefings about the progress of the investigation. Some sections in the political circle were upset about details tumbling out against terrorists belonging to the minority community. I argued in vain that terrorism did not have any religion and as police officers, it is our duty to follow leads and apprehend terrorists, irrespective of their faith. I knew that the repercussion of leaving a void for the media in such a critical case would be dangerous, as it could be filled with half-baked information, or even worse, false and concocted stories. This surely was a recipe for information disaster. Only time would tell the impact this would have on holding up information with the media.

8

IN THE EYE OF THE MEDIA STORM

22 September 2008

Everything was happening too quickly. Mohan's death left a void in the team and it was a tremendous setback to the Special Cell. Undeterred, everyone got immersed in collating further evidences and investigating the case, while the encounter itself was simultaneously being investigated by the South District police, as it came under its jurisdiction. Later, it was transferred to the Crime Branch.

Several leads needed to be chased. We had to work in a cohesive manner, examining all the findings and coordinating with intelligence agencies and various state police. I reviewed the progress made so far, including the examination of the evidence (both, physical and digital) recovered from Batla House and from the sites of the blasts and the CCTV footages.

Sanjeev shared that the electronic evidence recovered from L-18, Batla House was extracted expeditiously. Prima facie, they contained material to indoctrinate people into jihad, and some video clips and photographs of the bombs before they were planted for explosions.

Ravinder Tyagi played the CCTV footage of the area around Prince Paan Shop in M-Block Market, GK-1 just before the blast on 13 September. At 5.56 p.m., a person could be seen walking towards the shop. He was wearing a pair of blue jeans, a light-grey t-shirt with black stripes on the shoulder and a blue cap. He was seen carrying a red polythene bag in his right hand. At 6.00 p.m., the footage captured the same man walking towards the wall where the dustbins were kept (where the bomb was planted). He was seen holding a cigarette in his right hand, while clutching the polybag in his left. Within minutes, the person walked away from the dustbins, but without the polybag in his hand. At 6.30 p.m., a huge explosion is seen on the CCTV footage. All eyes were on this man now, and we believed he could be the one who planted the bomb. (Years later, Junaid was caught and he then confessed that the man seen on CCTV was indeed him and that he had planted the bombs there, which reconfirmed our initial finding.)

Sanjeev added that Shakeel, who was arrested by the South District police on 21st morning, had confessed that it was he who had planted the bomb in an autorickshaw in Karol Bagh. He then took a metro from Jhandewalan to Indraprastha and from there, he took an auto home. CCTV footage of the Jhandewalan Metro Station clearly showed Shakeel entering the station at 5.41 p.m. and then, he was seen near the ticket counter.

'Very good investigation, Sanjeev. And where are we on the post-mortem report of Atif and Sajid?' I was curious to know the results.

Inspector Sanjay Dutt informed that the post-mortem would be conducted in AIIMS today and the report is crucial. An important test called the dermal nitrate test will also be performed to determine whether the person has fired an firearm or not.[25] For this purpose, the doctor performing the post-mortem in cases of encounter deaths is requested by the investigating officer to collect the handwash of the deceased and send it for forensic examination.

After some time, I could see my staff officer HC Satender Singh in with a file containing newspaper clippings and reports. I started going through them one by one. I chanced upon one report that questioned the investigation of the different state police.

> *Who is the real mastermind? UP police made Waliullah of HuJI as the mastermind, while Shree P.C. Panday, D.G. of Gujarat, claimed that Abu Bashar and Tauqeer were the Indian Mujahideen mastermind behind the Gujarat and Jaipur blasts. On the contrary, the Delhi Police said that Atif was the Indian Mujahideen mastermind and caused the Gujarat, Jaipur, Delhi and UP blasts.[26]*

Many journalists had started comparing the statements of different police agencies and were claiming that they were conflicting. The statements of Additional Director General of Police (ADGP) UP and Director General of Police (DGP) Gujarat were based on the investigations done till the time they gave the statements, and further investigations had given more information unearthing the network of IM. While IM, supported by HuJI and the LeT, was the real operative, the logistics (i.e., the supply of RDX) before the arrest of Babu Bhai

---

[25]When a person fires from a firearm, the gunpowder residues are left on the hand from which firing is done. Therefore, the presence of gunpowder residue on the hands is an important piece of evidence to eliminate or prove if a person has used a firearm.

[26]'Who Is the Real Mastermind? UP, Gujarat Top Cops Refute Delhi Police Claim on Atif', *Mail Today*, 22 September 2008.

were provided by HuJI, confirming the statement of ADGP UP. In the Gujarat blasts, logistics were provided by SIMI, thereby confirming the statement given by DGP Gujarat. Therefore, the statements were not contradictory to each other, rather it was built on each state police's subsequent discoveries and evidence.

On the afternoon of 24 September, Alok rushed to my office with a newspaper in his hands. He seemed very upset. 'Sir, please see this story.' He handed over the newspaper to me. The newspaper claimed to have located two eyewitnesses who had anonymously shared a version of the encounter that rebut the account given by the Delhi Police. These eyewitnesses apparently observed the sequence of events from the bathroom of a flat near L-18, Batla House. They claimed to have inside view of Flat no. 108, located on the fourth floor, and the staircase of the building. They told the media that a member of the Special Cell first went up to the flat, but landed into an argument with one of the inmates. Hearing this, the other members of the police team rushed upstairs and dragged the two men down, and in the scuffle, Mohan got the bullet injury. Thereafter, the police team killed both the residents and dragged them up to the fourth floor along the stairs while Mohan was taken to the hospital. According to eyewitnesses, Atif and Sajid were unarmed. Their bodies were then wrapped in a cloth and taken away. Thereafter, the police team brought three persons, including Mohamad Saif, from somewhere around or within L-18. The story further claimed that the media has got the post-mortem reports of Sajid, Atif and Mohan and that as per the report, Mohan had got three bullets from the back which were fired from a close range not more than a few centimetres away. The article went on to say that the doctors performing the post-mortem attributed the injury marks on Atif and Sajid to a violent physical assault.

'This is false and baseless,' I told Alok after reading the news. I was following newspapers and getting intelligence inputs from the Batla House area. People in the area had started raising questions on how the Delhi Police could solve the blast cases within a week, while the cases in other states such as Jaipur and Hyderabad remained unsolved. As time passed, the versions got wilder and some people questioned why Jamia Nagar was the target when the actual culprits were hiding in the areas such as South Extension and Prithvi Raj Road.

What did it mean? Who was being referred to? I couldn't understand. If people knew of terrorists holed up in other areas, shouldn't they come forward with the information?

Assad Ghazi, an NGO worker, claimed that this was a move to counter the Rashtriya Swayamsevak Sangh (RSS)-BJP stand that the Centre was soft on terror, as elections were just a few months away.[27] Opinions on religious and political lines were being spread as 'deep, fact-based insights'.

Journalists started visiting the lanes and by-lanes of the Batla House area to fish out some interesting stories and perspectives. They heard gossips and rumours, which were unsupported by any evidences. However, some journalists picked up such stories and made no efforts to verify the authenticity of the source and started publishing in the newspapers and visual media. It seemed like neighbourhood gossip was being presented as 'news' by leading dailies and channels without any effort at fact-finding.

Alok said, 'I am also following these mischievous and misleading stories. But I don't give too much importance to them. But this story is upsetting. I cannot believe that such

---

[27]TNN, 'Mood Swung from Dazed to Angry', *The Times of India*, 20 September 2008. Available at: https://timesofindia.indiatimes.com/city/delhi/Mood-swung-from-dazed-to-angry/articleshow/3504971.cms. Last accessed on 24 July 2020.

absurd story can come out in a newspaper.'

'My worst fears are coming true, Alok. The media is developing stories weaving in quotes from people. Since the media is not getting direct quotes from the government agencies, they do not have access to our findings and investigation,' I responded and my anguish was visible.

We discussed and analysed the points raised in the article.

Claim 1: Two eyewitnesses claimed that they witnessed activity from the bathroom of their flat.

Fact: This was not valid. Alok and I had climbed to the rooftop of L-18 and also checked Flat no. 107 after the encounter. L-18 is a four-storied building, while the adjoining one are two storied. There is no scope to see inside Flat no. 108 from the bathroom of Flat no. 107.

Claim 2: Boys were shot on the ground floor and dragged upstairs.

Fact: If the boys were shot on the ground floor and thereafter dragged up to the fourth floor, there should have been blood stains or marks on the stairs of L-18, but there were none. Similarly, the bodies of both Atif and Sajid had no such drag marks.

Claim 3: Mohan got three bullet injuries from the back.

Fact: According to the post-mortem report, Mohan had two bullet injuries, both from front. Later, during the investigation, forensic report had established that Mohan got bullet injuries from bullets that were fired from a distance of one metre or more, demolishing the versions of close-range firing from a few centimetres.

Claim 4: The doctor after seeing Atif's post-mortem report has opined that he got injuries due to a scuffle and a violent assault.

Fact: This was a misleading depiction of the post-mortem report. Nowhere in the report has the doctor given this opinion. There is no injury which can be attributed to violence. (It was subsequently confirmed by the forensic team.)

Claim 5: It also says that Atif or Sajid didn't fire.

Fact: Atif and Sajid's handwash samples were collected to verify if they had fired or not and reports of the dermal nitrate test, which was awaited, would affirm or reject this claim. (Later on, the dermal nitrate test of both of them had come out positive thereby proving that they had fired on the police team.)

Claim 6: Saif was not involved and all of them were students.

Fact: The Maharashtra Police had arrested five IM members, and they all have corroborated the version given by Saif, thereby confirming his involvement along with Atif, Sajid and others arrested by the Delhi Police. Therefore, the insinuation made by the news item that Saif was falsely implicated gets disproved with the findings of the Mumbai Police also.

'All the evidence we have clearly indicates the genuineness of police action. However, we need to find some mechanism to dissuade the media from publishing unverified stories and encourage them to fact-check. My worry is that since elections are coming up, this will get more political,' I told Alok.

'I am also following the political debate on terrorism. Leading parties have strong opinions on this matter and the debate is being covered in the news,' Alok knew how it was being played out in the media with a political tangent.

Alok was right. The blasts in Delhi took place on 13 September. During this time, the political parties were developing strategy for the Lok Sabha elections, which were slated for early 2009. The national executive meet of the BJP was in progress from 12–14 September 2008. Their discussions were focussed on the upcoming assembly elections in five states—Delhi, Chhattisgarh, Madhya Pradesh, Mizoram and Rajasthan—around November–December, and the General Elections the next year. Shri Advani and Gujarat Chief Minister Shri Narendra Modi were already advocating for stringent anti-terrorism laws.

Shri Advani was about to address a public rally in Bangalore when he received the news of the serial blasts in Delhi. He rebuked the central government for not having an appropriate course of action to handle terrorism. He announced that the BJP would bring in POTA within 100 days of coming into power.

On 13 September, the Congress organized a meeting in Delhi to discuss the electoral strategy. Prime Minister Shri Manmohan Singh had stressed the importance of dealing with issues of terrorism, Naxalism and insurgency.

However, on 14 September, Patil, the then Union Home Minister, ruled out the possibility of enacting POTA. Shri Pranab Mukherjee, the then External Affairs Minister, added that, 'There is no dearth of laws in the country. It is a question of effectiveness of their implementation.'

'Sir, on 22 September, Atif's and Sajid's bodies were accompanied by the Shahi Imam of Jama Masjid from the Trauma Centre to the burial ground. He raised suspicion on how Mohan died and also claimed that one of the boys (terror accused) was shot in cold blood. His exact words were, "I cannot understand how a 17-year-old boy, a student of the 11th standard, can plot with Osama Bin Laden and spread terrorism",' Alok was furious on reading the false statement by the Imam.

'Well, we can only share the truth, data and evidence with all of them, but cannot address the misconstrued opinions that have already been formed. Sometimes, they believe what they want to believe even if the truth is right in front of them. We need to keep track of the political developments and ensure false news do not derail the investigation. Alok, prepare an electronic and physical folder of all evidences that we have collected so far. Let us keep them handy. It may be of help in responding to people's questions.'

I got a call from Sanjeev in the evening. He briefed me about the investigation at Manipal. 'During the interrogation, Saif had disclosed that he, along with one of his associates, Mohamad Khalid, had gone to Udupi, Karnataka, on 28 August 2008 to procure the explosive material from someone named Shahrukh. On 22 September, a team of the Special Cell took Saif to Karnataka, wherein he led the team to a hotel, New Broadways International Manipal, where they had stayed. The hotel staff has identified Saif as the same person who had stayed in the hotel along with one more person. Saif stayed there under the fake name Rahul Sharma and filled the hotel register in his own handwriting. The hotel's register and receipt of the room rent have been seized. The team could also locate the three PCOs used by Saif to call Shahrukh, from whom they received the explosive material for the Delhi blasts,' Sanjeev's excitement in giving out details about his investigation was palpable.

'Good work, Sanjeev! The pieces of the jigsaw puzzles are finally coming together,' I complimented him.

But amidst our investigation, some politicians had different agenda to follow.

I was sitting in my office one day when I saw Alok, Sanjeev and a few other officers visibly upset. They said that some politicians were trying to take advantage of the situation for vote bank politics. Shri Amar Singh, a leading politician of the

Samajwadi Party, was making allegations against the police. On the one hand, this leader had sent a cheque of ₹10 lakh to Mohan's family, and on the other hand, was alleging the encounter to be fake. Disturbed by the false allegations made by Shri Singh, Ms Maya Devi, Mohan's wife, refused to accept any financial help from him and returned the cheque.[28]

'Mohan's wife took a strong stand by not accepting any help from him due to his doublespeak,' I said.

One of the news items pointed out that a senior Congress leader, Shri Digvijay Singh, was also demanding an enquiry into the authenticity of the encounter.

'Sir, this is so discouraging. Do they want to fix us for their political mileage? If we fail in apprehending the terrorists, we are blamed for inefficiency and if we succeed, we have to face false allegations like these,' Sanjay was fuming.

I could see that these men who were working day in, day out in the service of the nation, putting their lives in danger without a second thought, were hurt, and rightfully so. Instead of supporting the police at this crucial time, they were being questioned. 'I understand your anguish and share the same sentiments. It is good to express it. When there is a storm in the ocean, a ship's captain does not anchor the ship, as any soft support is of no use. Instead, he fights out the storm. We have to fight this out, and we *will*. Our only chance to survive is to work harder and unearth as many evidences as possible. We know we are on the right track. The Maharashtra Police has arrested five members of this group confirming our findings that Atif and others were indeed involved in the terror activities.

---

[28]ET Bureau, 'Inspector Sharma's Family Returns Cheque to Amar Singh,' *The Economic Times*, 7 October 2008. Available at: https://economictimes.indiatimes.com/news/politics-and-nation/inspector-sharmas-family-returns-cheque-to-amar-singh/articleshow/3568084.cms. Last accessed on 14 June 2020.

Police teams of various states are also working equally hard. Let's hope that more terrorists of this group are caught soon. We already have ample evidences to prove our case to whoever truly wants to know the truth. We should not be disheartened. Like they say—tough times don't last, but tough people do. And you all are the toughest people I know.'

◆

Thereafter, I met with the CP and briefed him about the various developments including the apprehensions of the Special Cell team. He understood the issues we were facing. I also recommended that we send a proposal to the government to confer the Ashok Chakra[29] on Mohan. He agreed and called the lieutenant governor (LG), who also gave his consent. A proposal to this effect was sent to the central government. I was happy that there was some glimmer of hope in these tough times.

But I was restless that night. We had strict instructions from the Home Ministry to not attend any press conferences. An encounter had taken place in the capital, where all the media houses are based. Naturally, this was a big event for the media and they were hungry for information, running after elusive leads and instead banking on unconfirmed exclusive news from their 'sources'. The media was demanding information, but we had strict orders not to divulge investigation leads with them. So, there was a chaos. I can say for sure that the Delhi Police was losing its battle of perception. Something needed to be done. *But what?* And then, as if on some divine cue, my phone rang. It was 1.00 a.m. I knew this reporter. *What could be so urgent that she is calling at this time?*

---

[29]The Ashoka Chakra is the peacetime equivalent of the Param Vir Chakra and is awarded for the most conspicuous act of bravery, an act of daring, pre-eminent valour or self-sacrifice in the face of the enemy.

'Sir, sorry to bother you at this hour,' she was polite in her conversation.

'It's okay. I was still working.'

'I know what you are going through. My husband is an editor with a news channel and he will be able to guide you in how to tackle the media. I am handing over the phone to him.' Her husband requested for a meeting at a common place.

An appointment was fixed for the next morning at a mutually agreed place, but not in our offices. I, along with Alok, went to meet him. He had already prepared a handwritten 10-page note to guide me. His pointers were very useful.

We started communicating with people who could help in reaching out to editors of news channels and newspapers, to ensure they carry out correct versions and take into account the data and evidence *we* had. Communication and transparency was key.

I remember one such communication with Dr Naresh Trehan, a cardiovascular and cardiothoracic surgeon who was known to me for a long time and requested him to put in a word to some of the editors in the media. He used his resources and, by evening, a few senior journalists from the media (including the section of the media that was publishing unverified news items) came to meet me in my office. There was a volley of clarifications that they needed. I responded to each and every query with evidences, which made them understand the true facts of the case. I also told them that I was a phone call away and would be happy to respond to any questions. Thereafter, things started moving in the right direction in the media. At least the initial bias of the media against the Delhi Police was taken care of.

◆

On 3 October 2008, I was discussing the latest developments with some of the journalists. They apprised me that the vice chancellor (VC) of Jamia Millia, Professor Mushirul Hasan, had made a statement that the university would provide legal aid to its students arrested by the police after the encounter. I expressed that it was absolutely shocking. He (a public servant) was heading a university and should have shown more accountability and responsibility towards the society and the government. How could he think of providing legal aid to terrorists? This may create a perception in the minds of the community and the students that they were wronged by the police.

I was still in shock over the VC's actions when Alok came to my office. 'Sir, a petition has been filed in the Delhi High Court against the Special Cell. The high court has directed the police to allow Zia-ur-Rehman and Saqib Nissar to meet their relatives and advocates in the evening and made it clear that the police have to provide similar access to other persons arrested in the case. The high court has also directed that the police can remain present beyond the listening distance,' he told me with a degree of caution.

'Which means that the police should not know about the conversation between them. We should provide access as directed by the high court. I also want to meet the VC of Jamia Millia to explain to him about the incident. Please seek an appointment with him. What are the issues raised in the writ petition, Alok?'

'Mainly related to D.K. Basu Guidelines. We will respond to the allegations in our reply as the team has followed all the guidelines strictly.'

Later, Alok informed me that Senior Advocate Shri Prashant Bhushan and Zia-ur-Rehman's family members had visited the

Special Cell and met Zia-ur-Rehman. When Mr Bhushan came out of the Special Cell office, the media asked him questions, to which he replied, 'He [Zia] couldn't reveal anything concrete, Zia looked apparently okay. He seemed nervous, but the family is relieved now that they have met him.'

Alok also confirmed that the meeting with the VC had been scheduled in the afternoon of 6 October.

On 4 October 2008, Shri Dadwal called and asked me to accompany him to the Home Secretary's office. Generally, Shri Dadwal would have meetings with the Home Secretary. He would always prepare well so that he never required another officer to accompany him to the meetings. Till then, he had been managing the Batla House issue himself with the LG and the Ministry of Home Affairs. This was the first time that he wanted me to be with him.

I could understand that the political scenario was surcharged because of the forthcoming elections. Strong policies were needed to handle terrorism with an iron hand, with a clear indication that terrorism in any form would not be tolerated at any cost. Within the UPA, some leaders were demanding a judicial probe into the encounter and calling the encounter as fake.

The Special Cell had already prepared a dossier containing documentary and electronic evidences. I carried the material with me. When we reached the chamber of the Home Secretary, we saw that Shri Gopal Subramanium, the Additional Solicitor General, was already present there. The Home Secretary started discussing about the judicial inquiry. The commissioner expressed his opposition on the grounds that there were evidences to confirm that the group was involved in a number of terrorist activities across India. It was established not only by the Delhi Police but by independent investigation by other state police forces as well. I told him that I was carrying a plethora of evidences. I stressed that the team had gone there to perform their legal duties, to arrest the suspected terrorists. It was the terrorists who opened fire first at the police team. The police returned fire only in self-defense and in the process, we lost our own officer and another got a bullet injury, while the third survived the bullets as he was wearing a bullet-proof vest. Any order for judicial probe when incriminating evidences that were already at hand would deter investigating agencies in nabbing the terrorists. At this stage, Shri Subramanium intervened vociferously, emotionally expressing that he had seen the recoveries made by the Delhi Police Special Cell (Shri Subramanium was representing the Special Cell in the Supreme Court). The recoveries clearly brought out that they were indeed terrorists. He further emphasized that he had personally gone through the evidences, spoken to the police officers and the people from the locality, and was absolutely convinced that the encounter was genuine. Due to Shri Subramanium's intervention and the availability of a number of evidences, the Home Secretary decided to defer the matter.

During the same day, Shri Amar Singh visited Batla House and raised his demand for judicial probe into the encounter. He further asked that the then Home Minister be removed from office for not handling the Batla House issue appropriately. He threatened to withdraw his support to the UPA government. However, the Congress spokesperson, Manish Tiwari, took a balanced approach and said, 'It is extremely inappropriate for a political party to take a stand on any police action, either in support or in opposition.'

On the afternoon of 6 October, Alok and I proceeded to Jamia Millia University to meet its VC, Professor Hasan. We decided to commute in a private car to avoid undue attention.

I explained in detail about the activities of the residents of Flat no.108, L-18, Batla House. The evidences collected from the laptops and Atif's mobile phone were shown to him. After seeing the evidences, he was taken aback. He appeared to be convinced of their involvement in terrorism. Following that, he made no efforts or comments in support of the students involved in terror-related activities. I appreciated that the VC took time out to understand the issue with an open mind.

I ended my day by visiting Mohan's family along with my wife, Renuka. His family was under tremendous emotional turmoil. Their pain was increased manifold by the false narratives painted in media reports.

Without mincing words, Mohan's wife, Maya, candidly asked me. 'Sir, some people are saying that the encounter was fake.' She had tears in her eyes. 'Mohan had full faith in you, sir. I want to know the truth from you. Was the encounter really fake?'

'The encounter was genuine. The boys who died and the ones who were arrested were indeed terrorists.' I waited for her reaction and could see peace dawning on her face.

It goes to Maya's credit that she exhibited extraordinary balance and unwavering conviction. She was offered an election ticket in the forthcoming Delhi Assembly Elections, but she declined.[30] She only wanted justice for her martyred husband, Mohan.

[30]Suman K Jha, 'Slain Cop MC Sharma's Wife Turns Down BJP Offer of Ticket', *The Indian Express*, 9 November 2008. Available at: http://archive.indianexpress.com/news/slain-cop-mc-sharma-s-wife-turns-down-bjp-offer-of-ticket/383659/. Last accessed on 14 June 2020.

9

NO ONE IS ABOVE THE LAW

The Special Cell and the police teams of the other states had done their duty towards the nation, towards the society by fighting against terrorism. Mohan sacrificed his life at the altar of his duties, like so many other unsung heroes do every day. And here we were, engulfed by vote bank politics, media TRPs and conspiracy theorists. The lack of a political consensus on how to deal with terrorism had made it difficult to have stringent policies to tackle it.

It seemed like we were living in a world with divided media and public opinion. In one realm, our department, the Special Cell, was the biggest villain, compromising human rights. In their eyes, we were doing everything wrong. The other realm comprising of majority of the public and media people was deeply appreciative and supportive of our work. A number of people reached out to me personally to thank me and the Special Cell team for the work we were doing to root out terrorism. Their words encouraged and motivated us to continue our work against terrorism without worrying about the criticism. At the same time, the adverse comments by the media and politicians demoralized the team. *Why can't we keep politics out of it for once and fight the menace of terrorism like one united nation?*

The Batla House encounter issue was also put on a public trial. On 12 October 2008, a group of teachers from Jamia Millia Islamia set up a *jan sunwai* (public hearing), on the Batla House encounter. The jury comprised politician and social activist Swami Agnivesh, human rights and political activist John Dayal and Delhi University professors Tripta Wahi, Vijay Singh and Nirmalangshu Mukherji. More than a dozen Jamia residents gave testimonies at that meeting. Relatives of Atif as well as those who knew Sajid spoke in front of the jury. Later, the jury gave its findings, which were basically a repetition of what had appeared in some media reports and were already addressed and answered by us. The questions raised in the hearing were:

- *How many masterminds were there?*
- *Atif was never mentioned by the police till then, so how can he suddenly become the new mastermind?*
- *The police could have asked them to surrender without entering the flat, did they do that?*
- *Why did Mohan not wear a bullet-proof jacket?*
- *How could two people escape?*
- *How could the police claim so early on that they were terrorists?*
- *Why would they submit the correct address in the police station in the tenant verification form (while taking the Flat no. 108, L-18, Batla House on rent)?*
- *Why were the post-mortem reports not made public?*

Most of the queries (except the one about the post-mortem reports) were similar to those raised by journalists during the press conferences we held earlier. I had already responded to each one of them. The post-mortem reports were given to the persons permitted by law.

Their findings were devoid of merit and none of the people who deposed in the *jan sunwai* had first-hand knowledge of the event. That is the reason why none of them subsequently came forward to share these testimonies or gave any affidavit in the high court or the Supreme Court.

On 14 October, a new dimension was given to the Batla House encounter when a few senior politicians from Minority Department, Indian National Congress, decided to send a delegation to meet Congress president Mrs Sonia Gandhi and PM Dr Manmohan Singh to raise a complaint against 'the injustice done to Muslims' and to urge a judicial probe into the encounter. Shri Kapil Sibal, minister for science and technology, along with other political leaders visited the Batla House area before meeting Mrs Gandhi and Dr Singh.

On the same day, Shri Mulayam Singh Yadav, the founder-patron of the Samajwadi Party, and Shri Amar Singh met Dr Singh to ask for a judicial enquiry. Political pressure was building up from all sides.

Shri Amar Singh visited the Jamia Nagar area to address a huge gathering on 17 October. He was accompanied by Ms Mamata Banerjee of the All India Trinamool Congress. I watched their speeches in the news. She believed the encounter was fake and the terror accused were targeted because of their religion. She set a 72-hour deadline for the government to direct a judicial enquiry and asserted that she would not give up till the demands were met.

Shri Amar Singh also spoke to the gathering and pointed out that Mohan was not wearing a bullet-proof jacket. *'Encounter specialist bina bullet-proof jacket aa gaye, hur jagah jacket pahanni thi pur khudkashi karne aa gaye.* (The encounter expert came without a bullet-proof jacket, he wore the jacket everywhere, but here he came to commit suicide).' When he said this, the audience clapped and cheered. *How insensitive this statement was!* He also mentioned that he had proposed to donate ₹10 lakh to Mohan's wife, Maya Sharma. He gave the reason for his proposal, *'Goli chahe kisi ki lagi ho, mare toh.* (The bullet that hit him could have been anyone's, but he is dead).' The people could be heard laughing and clapping. *'Aur unko mera sukraguzar hona chahiye, unki khawind ki maut ka asli katil kaun hain uski taswij karne ki baat kar raha hoon.* (And she should be grateful to me for asking to find out the real killer of her husband).' The roar and laughter of the people was a mockery on the tragedy that had befallen on the family of a slain police officer.

What did he mean by finding the real killer of her husband? Mohan was martyred in a mission for his country. I was astonished at the speed at which controversies were being spun out of thin air.

On the other side, the BJP was hitting out at Shri Singh and Ms Banerjee for engaging in vote bank politics on an issue of national security. The BJP had decided to make national security its pivotal agenda for the upcoming elections.

Pressure was mounting on the government from all fronts. It was being accused of going soft on terror. The Opposition was advocating stringent action against the terrorists and supporting the police force working in counterterrorism. The government decided to take stock of the evidences available with the Delhi Police Special Cell. The next morning, the LG of Delhi, Shri Khanna, rang me and said that Shri Sibal wanted to discuss the issues related to the encounter. While putting down the phone, he advised me, 'Come prepared.'

I asked Alok to send Ravinder along with the laptop containing all the evidences. Both of us went to Shri Khanna's residence. I carried the laptop with me into the room where

Shri Khanna and Shri Sibal were sitting. I greeted them and sat across from Shri Sibal. Shri Khanna was seated at the other end, intently observing the deliberations between Shri Sibal and me.

Shri Sibal brought out the newspaper clippings one by one and asked me to explain the various issues that were raised. I responded to every issue and shared the information that was available with the police, the topography of the area as well as that of Flat no. 108, L-18, Batla House. I further explained how the teams went in. I drew a blueprint of the flat to explain how the encounter went down. We went into details of the positions of the police officers and the terrorists. Many issues were addressed during this conversation. I explained how Sajid got bullet injuries on the head, and I clarified the controversy raised in the media about the post-mortem reports.

'Sir, if you permit me, can I show you the materials recovered from L-18, Batla House? This will show their involvement in terrorist activities,' I requested him.

'Sure. Please go ahead.'

'We have recovered the electronic material from the memory card and mobile phone belonging to Atif. We have also found mobile phones of the others staying at L-18, two pen drives, two laptops and around 40 CDs. They contain video clips and photographs related to the Ahmedabad, Jaipur and Delhi blasts. Please have a look, sir.' I pointed to a photograph and video of the Ahmedabad blasts.

In the photograph, bombs were arranged in letters I and M for 'India Mujahideen' and were placed on a bed, while a cloth piece that read 'Indian Mujahideen Ahmedabad' was hanging behind them. The same was shown in more details in a video. Three other photographs were of the cars used in the explosion in Ahmedabad, and one photograph was that of a car with the bomb planted in it. There was a video clip of a

Explosive devices arranged in the form of 'IM'. These bombs were later planted in Ahmedabad on 26 July 2008 .This picture was found in Atif Ameen's mobile phone.
(Part of the charge sheet relating to the bomb blast cases of 2008 filed in the court.)

bomb on a bicycle with frame no. 129489 placed near Kotwali in Jaipur, one video clip of a dustbin placed in M-Block Market, Greater Kailash-1 in Delhi and one video clip of a dustbin at the children's park in Delhi.

'Sir, these video clips and photographs are of bombs before the blasts and cannot be found with anyone but those who were actually involved in these explosions.'

I could see that he was taking an interest in it. I continued, 'They were travelling with fake names, sir.'

I showed him the forged identity cards. There was a fake driving licence in the name of Farhat, but the photograph was that of Atif. Another driving licence was in the name of Mohd. Razique with Atif's photograph. A forged Election Commission card and driving licence, both in the name of Pankaj Sharma, had Sajid's photograph on them. A forged driving licence and Election Commission card, both in the name Rahul Sharma, were with the photograph of Mohamad Saif. Saif's photograph was also there on a driving licence found in the name of Sameer Khan. There were several other identity proofs that were forged for other members of their group. An election card in the name of Ajay with Mohd. Shakeel's photo, an ID card of Symbiosis University in the name of Amir Talha with Zeeshan's photo and a driving licence in the name of Abdul Qari with Ariz Khan's photo were recovered. They were using fake names and identities. It was a false identity maze they had created.

Atif had taken admission in Jamia Millia University based on a forged degree. Evidences pertaining to their travel to Ahmedabad and Jaipur were also shown to Sibal. They also travelled to Jaipur and Ahmedabad with fake names at the time of explosions in these areas. Mohamad Saif travelled with a fake name to Manipal to collect explosives from there. I showed him various other evidences available in the electronic media.

I also addressed the issue raised by Sajid's family and some of the local leaders about his age—he was only 17 years old—and that he could not have been involved in terrorist activities. They were insinuating that an innocent minor had been killed by the Delhi Police in the encounter. Their statement was covered by some of the newspapers. This led to a complaint to the Delhi Commission for Protection of Child Rights, which in turn, asked for a response from the Delhi Police. A driving licence and an Election Commission card in his name with his photograph were also seized from Batla House. On verification these documents were found to be genuine. They revealed Sajid's age to be 23, and not 17.

I was not done yet. 'Sir, the recovered electronic data also contains a PowerPoint presentation based on the Gujarat riots, and a few other countries. There are excerpts from jihadi books and Osama Bin Laden's speech, along with songs and chants motivating people to join jihad.' I played some of the songs from our digital evidence. All of us listened to the evidence in complete silence.

At the end of the discussion, I also shared that the Maharashtra Police had arrested 20 members of IM, while the UP Police had arrested one. All of them had corroborated the findings of the Delhi Police.

It was more than an hour-long discussion and questioning. During this period, Shri Khanna did not intervene but was observing the proceedings. At the end, Shri Sibal admitted that he was convinced of the genuineness of the encounter and of the accused being involved in terrorist activities. He agreed to convey the same to Dr Singh. He took my number and true to his words, he rang me in the evening to confirm that he had conveyed what he found during discussions to the PM.

Subsequently, the government took a strong stand and

refused any judicial probe. It decided to let the law take its course in the high court, the Supreme Court and the NHRC.

A few days later, I was sitting in office, when a breaking news flashed on the television screen.

'Joint Commissioner of the Special Cell shunted out.'

I looked at the news in amusement and recalled a conversation I had with the CP just a couple of days before.

'Karnal, you have spent almost five years in the Special Cell, handling terrorism. I know it is a very challenging and demanding posting. Looking at your career trajectory and future prospects, I believe you will benefit from Range posting[31].' These were the CP's words to me.

'Sir, you can post me anywhere you feel my expertise and skills will be utilized the best. Although, I am not sure Range is the right step after the Special Cell.' This was more in the nature of a query, rather than a reservation.

'At some point, you will be considered to become Commissioner of Police. It may come as a criticism at that time that you have not done any field posting at a Range level. So, it is good to get that experience looking at your overall career growth.'

'I agree, sir. I have a request though. Allow me to handle the proceedings in the NHRC, the high court and the Supreme Court relating to the Batla House encounter, as I am well conversant about the case.'

'Consider it done, Karnal.'

◆

After a few days, my transfer orders came for me to join as Joint Commissioner of Police (Northern Range) with additional

---

[31]A Joint CP/Range supervises the functioning of two to three districts. It is a field posting.

charge of the Special Cell. But of course the news channel decided to edit the news and present only a partial picture. I laughed it off. *How typical of the media to sensationalize this for their TRPs.*

I reached out to Rajan to convey to the press that I still held charge of the Special Cell and was not 'shunted out'. The scroll was immediately removed from the channel.

Our team was overwhelmed with the work of investigation, following leads to track the absconding terrorists on one hand and on the other hand it had to prepare and respond to queries from media, civil societies and politicians. In any encounter case, there should be one all-encompassing, comprehensive enquiry instead of so many. Concerned departments could come together for a review if needed. The Batla House incident was battling on several fronts. To begin with, senior officers conduct initial scrutiny to ensure that the version of the incident given by the team is genuine. I had visited Batla House immediately after the encounter and examined the scene, spoken to officers at the spot, those who were in the hospital with Mohan, and Balwant, who was in AIIMS. All of their versions were consistent. Second, the LG and the Home Ministry sought reports to assess and take appropriate stand. Third, the NHRC had called for the reports to examine the veracity of the encounter. Fourth, the Minority Commission had called for the report to satisfy itself about the encounter. Fifth, the investigation of the encounter was transferred to the Crime Branch, which was not under the control of the Special Cell. The Crime Branch would submit the report to the judicial magistrate after investigation, where it would get judicial scrutiny.

The Special Cell team had gone to arrest the people suspected to be involved in terrorist activities. They fired on the police team killing Mohan, injuring Balwant and almost killing

Rajbir. Subsequently, ample evidences were found against them not only by the Delhi Police but by other state police departments, too, confirming that they were indeed involved in a series of explosions in different cities, month after month. Still the team had to face a lot of criticism and scrutiny from several sections of the media and politicians.

However, now the legal battle had begun on the Batla House encounter. The Delhi Police was represented in the Delhi High Court by Ms Mukta Gupta, the then standing counsel, and her team. She is a thorough professional and would scrutinize each and every document and pose questions to me and my team so as to be absolutely sure of the facts of the case before filing any reply in the high court. A day before and on the day of the hearing, we would spend time with her discussing the nuances of the hearing.

Shri Subramanium, the then Additional Solicitor General of India, represented the Delhi Police in the Supreme Court. He is one of the country's leading lawyers and a wonderful orator. He would spend hours with us trying to understand every aspect of the case.

Every day was a challenge and some surprise or the other lay in store for us. On 1 October 2008, the General Secretary of Real Cause, an NGO at Jamia Nagar, Delhi, filed a writ petition before the Supreme Court requesting for a Central Bureau of Investigation (CBI) enquiry into the encounter. After hearing the petitioner, the Supreme Court dismissed the petition on 8 December 2008. But the NGO was persistent. It filed a review petition asking for the CBI enquiry. The Supreme Court's observation ended this episode then and there. It stated, 'We have gone through the review petition and the connected records. We do not find any merit in the same. The review petition is dismissed.'

In the Delhi High Court, two civil writ petitions were filed. The first petition was filed on 3 October 2008 alleging that the Delhi Police had not complied with the D.K. Basu Guidelines issued by the Supreme Court. In our reply, we gave details that illustrated strict adherence to these guidelines. The Delhi High Court disposed this petition on 22 January 2009.

The second writ petition was filed in the Delhi High Court by the social-cultural organization Act Now for Harmony and Democracy (ANHAD). This public interest litigation (PIL) contained the following prayers:

a) To direct the government to initiate a judicial enquiry into the encounter;

b) To direct the government to initiate an enquiry into which police officer permitted the *India Today* journalist to interview the accused while they were still in police custody;

c) To initiate a contempt proceeding against *India Today* and the said journalist for publishing confessional statements made by the accused before the police and, thereby, tending to prejudice the judicial proceedings;

d) To direct the police and the media to lay down the directions to be followed by them regarding the release or publication of information/evidence against the accused that was obtained by the police during interrogation/ investigation of the accused, when the matter is sub judice.

The petition cited a cover story, 'Inside the Mind of the Bomber', by journalist Mihir Srivastava that appeared in *India Today*.[32]

---

[32] Mihir Srivastava, 'Inside the Mind of the Bombers', *India Today*, 2 October 2008. Available at: https://www.indiatoday.in/magazine/cover-story/story/20081013-inside-the-mind-of-the-bombers-737793-2008-10-02. Last accessed on 16 June 2020.

Mihir was able to take the interview of the three accused (Zia-ur-Rehman, Saquib Nisar and Mohd. Shakeel) arrested by South District Police. He managed to get the interview with the help of a common friend of those arrested. In the interview, they all confessed taking part in terror activities without any remorse. Zia-ur-Rehman even told him, 'If Allah wants, I'll bomb the market where my mother buys vegetables. She will be sent to paradise.' This interview brought out the extent of radicalization done to them and their involvement in terror activities. The petition wanted that the Court should direct the media and the government to come out with a media policy.

We filed status reports from time to time as asked by the Delhi High Court. On 6 November 2008, the CP sent a report to the LG which contained details of the IM terror module, and all the facts pertaining to the encounter. Based on the report, the CP requested the LG to not order a magisterial enquiry into the encounter.

On 7 November 2008, the Delhi High Court observed:

We have heard the learned counsel appearing for both sides. We are informed that some complaints with respect to the incident of encounter in question have been filed before the National Human Rights Commission (NHRC) and in response to those complaints, the NHRC has asked for reports and the proceedings are pending before the NHRC.

We are also informed by Ms Mukta Gupta, Learned Standing Counsel, that a preliminary report by the Joint Commissioner of Police, Special Cell, Delhi has been forwarded to the NHRC and extension of time for filing a further detailed report has been sought. In the

circumstances, we are not inclined to express any opinion
at this stage in so far as prayer clause 'a' is concerned.
    As regards clause 'b' and 'd' are concerned, issue notice
to the respondents, returnable on 15 December 2008.

The Delhi High Court issued notice relating to the media policy.

At the end of December, I left charge of the Special Cell. CP asked me to continue coordinating with the officers of the Cell and the advocates for representation in the courts and the NHRC. It was my responsibility to handle the court matters despite my transfer. I stayed abreast of all the developments on this case in the courts.

In first week of January 2009, the CP called me to his office. 'Karnal, I had written a letter to the LG giving details of the Batla House encounter, evidences collected by the Special Cell and the progress of investigation by the Crime Branch. The LG wants you to explain the whole case to him. He has to take a decision on whether to order a magisterial enquiry.'

I went to the office of the LG, Shri Khanna. He had already read the detailed letter sent by the CP. He had also heard my discussion with Shri Sibal very intently. Therefore, he was well aware of the intricacies of the case. He sought further clarification.

Subsequently, the Deputy Secretary of the Government of Delhi submitted the decision of the LG declining a magisterial enquiry to the NHRC and the high court. The LG in his order first summarized the circumstances under which the encounter took place and then discussed the evidences against the IM group including Atif and Sajid, who were involved in terror attacks in various part of the country and who had died in the encounter.

LG finally observed that,

> ...in these circumstances, when the police went to apprehend
> the accused and they were fired upon, there was no option
> with them but to open fire in self-defense and to arrest
> the accused. The modules of the Indian Mujahideen have
> conducted bomb explosions in various parts of the country
> including Delhi, Uttar Pradesh, Rajasthan, Gujarat,
> Karnataka, Andhra Pradesh, etc. Subjecting police officers,
> who have worked out this case at the cost of losing a gallant
> colleague and nearly losing another, to a magisterial
> enquiry would be highly demoralizing and would weaken
> the resolve of the police officers to fight against terrorists.
> A police officer confronted by armed terrorists should not
> have to start thinking whether to die of the firing from the
> militants or if the militant dies to face the magisterial
> enquiries which are to follow. The Crime Branch is
> already conducting an investigation of the shootout. Two
> of the accused are yet to be arrested. The Crime Branch is
> expected to file its charge sheet in the Court shortly after
> which the case will be subjected to due judicial scrutiny.[33]

During this time, I received news that the Government had
decided to confer Ashok Chakra, the highest gallantry award,
to Mohan posthumously. On 26 January 2009 at Rajpath,
Smt Maya, Mohan's wife, received the award from President
Pratibha Patil. The ceremony was attended by thousands,
including foreign dignitaries. All of us in the Special Cell,
and his family, felt extremely proud of Mohan, but it
came with pangs of extreme grief that he was not with us
any more.

---

[33]It was the report submitted in NHRC and high court by the Dy. Secretary (Home)
Delhi and it is part of NHRC orders as well as of proceeding of the high court.

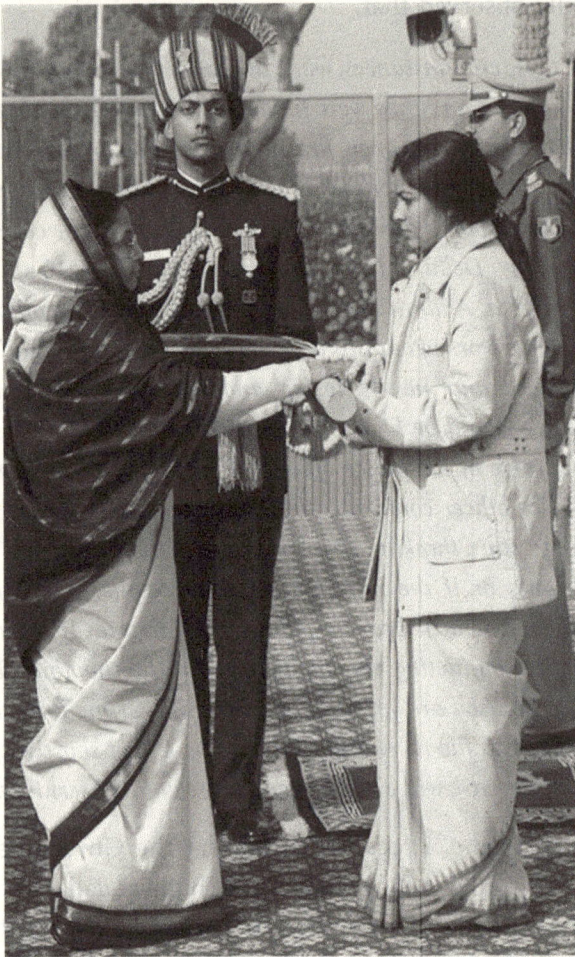

Smt Maya Sharma receiving the Ashok Chakra which was awarded to her husband Shri Mohan Chand Sharma (posthumous) from the President of India.
Image credit: https://commons.wikimedia.org/wiki/File:Smt._Maya_Sharma_receiving_Ashoka_Chakra_awarded_to_her_husband_Shri_Mohan_Chandra_Sharma_(Posthumous)_from_the_President,_Smt._Pratibha_Devisingh_Patil,_during_the_60th_Republic_Day_Parade-2009,_in_New_Delhi.jpg

On 16 February 1948, the Delhi Police got its first Inspector General of Police, D.W. Mehra (at that time IGP was the highest rank in a state police). On that date every year, the Delhi Police organizes its Raising Day commemoration. It is a week-long programme starting with the police parade in the New Police Lines, Kingsway Camp and culminating with the 'At Home' function on 22 February. In 2009, 'At Home' was organized in the New Police Lines grounds, Kingsway camp. This event was attended by the President, the PM, various dignitaries, police officers and their families. I attended this function with my wife, Renuka. During the function, we were walking towards the president to greet her. On the way, I noticed the LG was engaged in a discussion with the PM. On seeing me, he stopped me and introduced me to the PM. I greeted both of them. The LG praised me and remarked that I headed the team that cracked the case of IM. The PM looked at me and said, 'You have done a good job.' I heartily thanked both of them. As we walked away, I felt my heart warming up with happiness and satisfaction. I looked at my wife and saw her beaming with pride.

The last few months had been very hard on my family. Disturbing news articles and blogs, several ongoing legal battles and never-ending gossip and accusations in different circles had drained us. They would keep a strong face, but I knew their heart ached every time someone mentioned the encounter. People write and say a lot of hurtful things, without even knowing the authenticity of the event in question. As police officers, we develop a thick skin, but the well-being of our family members does get impacted.

One day, I got a call from my younger daughter, Kritika, who was away from home studying in Manipal University. 'Papa, one of my friends is saying that the high court is soon going to order an enquiry against you and the Special Cell.' She sounded anxious and sad.

'No, this is not true, Kritika,' I tried to calm her down.

'But, Papa, I have been reading some blogs and online news and they are writing awful things about you and your department. You are in such a thankless job, Papa. Will they crucify you for doing your job?'

My heart sank, but I shrugged it off and told her that this is a temporary phase. 'We have submitted reports to the high court and the NHRC. The Special Cell has done exceptionally good work in unravelling the identity of IM, which seemed to be unstoppable at one stage. My team has done nothing wrong. Some people may be spreading rumours against the Cell, but none of that is true. You shouldn't bother yourself with this. What is the view of your other friends?' I asked her.

She became jubilant, 'They have a very high opinion of you and the Special Cell.'

'Then be happy,' I replied. My concerned daughter was somehow pacified.

Then there were more developments on the legal front. On 22 May 2009, the Delhi High Court directed the NHRC to conduct an enquiry and submit its report. The NHRC conducted its enquiry and filed the report on 22 July. On 26 August, the high court gave its judgement, taking the NHRC's report into consideration. The NHRC's report had addressed all the issues that were raised on several fronts. The NHRC panel, which conducted the enquiry, comprised Acting Chairman of NHRC, Mr Justice G.P. Mathur (retired judge of the Supreme Court) and three members of the NHRC: Mr Justice B.C. Patel (retired as Chief Justice of the Delhi High Court), Shri Satyabrata Pal (retired Indian Foreign Service [IFS] officer of the 1972 batch) and Shri P.C. Sharma (former director of the CBI and an IPS officer of the 1966 batch).

To begin with, the commission formulated the scope of enquiry as follows:

The scope of enquiry before the commission is very limited. The only question which we propose to consider is whether the police opened fire without any justification or it had acted in the exercise of Right to self defence...

The commission considered the complaint made by Kamran Siddiqui, the General Secretary, Real Cause and the reports submitted to the commission by the Special Cell, vigilance and the Crime Branch of the Delhi Police and the report submitted by the deputy secretary (Home) of the Delhi government. The commission deliberated threadbare on the post-mortem reports of Mohan, Atif and Sajid; medico legal certificate (MLC) of Balwant; biological and serological report of CFSL; firearm examination report of CFSL, etc.

The commission noted that:

...It is noteworthy that Inspector Mohan Chand Sharma received injuries on the front portion of the body... The locus of firearm injuries found on the body of Inspector Mohan Chand Sharma corroborate the police version that a volley of bullets was fired on the police team as soon as it entered Flat No.108, L-18, Batla House through the side gate. HC Balwant Singh was also with Inspector Mohan Chand Sharma. He sustained firearm entry wound on the dorsal aspect of right arm and the bullet exited through his palm...

The commission observed that the firearm examination report confirmed that Rajbir, our HC, was hit with two bullets on his chest. These bullets hit his bullet-proof jacket and they were fired from the pistol lying in the room of Flat no. 108. Eight fired cartridge cases recovered from the flat were fired from the two .30 pistols recovered from the flat. Since the police doesn't possess .30 weapons, the commission deliberated on who could have used them.

Who then had used these pistols? The answer is provided by the firearms examination report. The swabs which were taken from the right hands of Mohd. Atif Ameen and Mohd. Sajid by the doctors at the time of postmortem in AIIMS were sent in sealed bottles to CFSL for dermal nitrate tests in the laboratory. The same were found to contain gunshot residue. This conclusively establishes that Mohd. Atif Ameen and Mohd. Sajid had both used firearms at the time of incident. It may be mentioned that the police had no role whatsoever, either in the taking of swabs from the hands of the two deceased or in the dermal nitrate tests of the same. The swabs were taken by the doctors in AIIMS and the tests were conducted in the laboratory of CFSL, CBI.

The commission thereafter examined the issued raised by Kamran Siddique and observed that:

The complainant sees something fishy about the injuries sustained by Inspector Mohan Chand Sharma. He has mentioned some photographs published in the print media which show blood on the left shoulder only. He has also referred to a report published in Mail Today on 24th September 2008 according to which, three shots were fired at Inspector Mohan Chand Sharma on the back. He has also alleged that serious differences had cropped up between the martyr Mohan Chand Sharma and another police officer namely Rajbir Singh, implying thereby that the death of Inspector Mohan Chand Sharma might be the result of intra departmental rivalry. All these doubts of the complainant have absolutely no basis. The postmortem report of Inspector Mohan Chand Sharma is conclusive proof of the fact that he had received a gunshot wound on the hypochondriac region of the abdomen which completely rules out an attack on him from the backside.

The complainant has posed a question as to why Inspector Mohan Chand Sharma went to Flat No.108 in plain clothes when he was fully aware that there were terrorists inside and why he did not use the bullet-proof jacket? It is quite likely that Inspector Mohan Chand Sharma did not consider it prudent to wear a bullet-proof jacket lest it may arouse suspicion and alert the alleged terrorists. It is also likely that he did not apprehend that the occupants of the flat would be having weapons and they will immediately resort to firing. There can be various reasons and it will not be proper to speculate as to why Inspector Mohan Chand Sharma did not wear a bullet-proof jacket.

The report went on...

The complainant also wants us to reject the theory of encounter because according to him, the police version regarding escape of two terrorists from the scene is totally unbelievable. He points out that the whole area was cordoned off and premises No. L-18, Batla House was heavily guarded by the police force and there being only one staircase in the building, it was not possible for any suspect to escape from the building. We are not inclined to examine this aspect in minute detail. As mentioned above, the enquiry is limited to the effect of the encounter. There

*are two doors in the flat in question and there are two flats
in each of the four floors. According to the police version, a
number of persons had gathered at the time of incident. In
the melee, it was possible for some persons to escape. At any
rate, the alleged escape of two persons can have no bearing
on the main incident in which Inspector Mohan Chand
Sharma received fatal gunshot injuries and HC Balwant
Singh also received grievous injuries and the action taken
by the police party in self-defense which resulted in death
of Mohd. Atif Ameen and Mohd. Sajid.*

The commission then concluded that:

*There can be no manner of doubt that firing was first
resorted to by the occupants of the room on the police party.
If the police party had first resorted to firing, the occupants
of the room namely Mohd. Atif Ameen and Mohd. Sajid
after receiving injuries from service weapons would have
immediately fallen down and would not at all have been
in any position to fire upon the police party. The fact that
Inspector Mohan Chand Sharma and HC Balwant Singh
received gunshot injuries leads to the only inference that
firing was first resorted to by occupants of the room.*

*...there is ample and sufficient material before us which
leads to the irresistible conclusion that there was imminent
danger to the life of members of the police party.*

The commission finally closed the enquiry concluding that:

*...the police party clearly acted in right of self-defense. In
such circumstances, the action taken by the police party is
fully protected by law.*

During the proceeding in the high court when the NHRC report was being discussed, Mr Prashant Bhushan, senior advocate in the Supreme Court, tried to dispute the conclusion arrived at by the NHRC and sought a fresh independent judicial enquiry by a retired Supreme Court judge. However, the high court concluded the matter by stating that:

> *Keeping in view the aforesaid findings as well as the fact that the NHRC is a high-powered statutory body comprising of retired Supreme Court and High Courts judges and the fact that we are examining the present petition in Article 226 jurisdiction, we are of the opinion that the report of the NHRC calls for no interference. Consequently, we reject the prayer 'a' of the writ petition by which an independent judicial inquiry had been sought into the said encounter.*

Thereafter, the petitioner ANHAD approached the Supreme Court against the order of the Delhi High Court. The apex court dismissed the request a year after the incident.

With this order, the judicial scrutiny of the encounter finally came to an end. The highest court in the country had given its verdict and cleared the Special Cell of all charges that the Batla House encounter was fake.

Although the NHRC report and the verdict of the high court and the Supreme Court were very comprehensive, the Batla House encounter continues to be referenced in political speeches during elections and in TV debates till date.

It is disheartening that although more than a decade has elapsed since the Batla House encounter, it has been debated during all the Assembly and general elections ever since. I wonder when the ghosts of the Batla House conspiracies will die.

As the sound and fury of these debates overwhelmed the living rooms and election rallies, we silently continued with our investigations in unravelling the mystery of IM.

10

THE GENESIS OF INDIAN MUJAHIDEEN

Theories and counter theories. This has been the life of IM in this country. Sceptics and permanent contrarians have, for reasons best known to them, raised doubts about the existence of IM. Over the course of our investigations, interrogations and extensive research, we have deciphered how IM came into being, its path and evolution.

This is their story.

IM had announced its existence with a bang when it sent an email to the media, minutes before the blasts in UP courts, in 2007. The intelligence and anti-terror investigating agencies were until then unaware of the existence of any terror outfit by this name. It had proved to be one of the most lethal terror outfits so far.

The story of IM begins with one man, Asif Raza Khan, and his quest to join a jihadi outfit.

Asif, born in 1971 in Kolkata, graduated in 1992 from the Maulana Azad College, Kolkata. During his school and college days, he came under the influence of the Tablighi Jamaat, a conservative religious group which is a derivative of the Deobandi movement. It was formed by Maulana Muhammad

Ilyas in 1926 with the aim of elevating the declining values of Islam, something that was deemed as a threat to Muslims. It consistently grew from a local to a national to finally an international movement with presence in 200 countries and with over 10 million followers. Their tasks are coordinated through their headquarters called Markaz. They have an international headquarter in South Delhi called the Nizamuddin Markaz.[34]

Due to his indoctrination, Asif was branded as a Wahhabi.[35] Asif started following news items related to communal riots taking place in various parts of the country. In 1989, he started attending the weekly Ijtema, a religious congregation organized by SIMI where lectures and discussions are held on the Holy Quran and its signification in order to achieve salvation. However, he soon dissociated himself from SIMI and joined the Students Islamic Organisation of India (SIO), which is a moderate Muslim students' wing of Jamaat-e-Islami Hind (JIH). Formed in 1982, SIO's mission is to organize activities to engage youth in peaceful religious activities. He was not satisfied with the functioning of SIO and left this as well.

Thereafter, he deliberated with his close associates about initiating violent action against Hindu fundamentalists. He knew they needed proper training of arms and ammunition to achieve their goal. During the late 1980s and the early '90s, militancy was on the rise in J&K. He actively searched for a contact in Kashmir to approach the militants there. A Kashmiri named Yaseen Khan used to come to Kolkata to sell Kashmiri shawls. Asif cultivated him and started discussing with him about militancy in Kashmir. Asif projected himself as a member

---

[34]This Markaz was in the news recently when during the Coronavirus pandemic, a huge congregation had gathered at its headquarters.
[35]The Wahhabi group is one of most conservative Islamic groups founded in the eighteenth century.

of the Islamic Commando Force (a fictitious name). Yaseen agreed to introduce him to a militant in Kashmir. Asif made his first visit to Kashmir in 1991, where he met a person named Sanaullah, who was the talent spotter for Hizbul Mujahideen (HM). Asif requested him to send him to Pakistan for arms training. His request was declined citing strict vigil on the Indo-Pak border.

But Asif was adamant. He, along with two members of his group, visited Kashmir again in June 1992. This time, he met Gulam Mohammad, who had replaced Sanaullah. Gulam arranged a short-term arms training on handling AK-47 rifles, pistols and lobbing of grenades. Gulam further coordinated their meeting with Syed Salahuddin (head of HM in Kashmir), who was escorted by around 50 HM militants armed with grenades, AK-47 rifles and rocket-propelled grenades (RPG). Salahuddin also carried a walkie-talkie with him. Asif requested Salahuddin to send them to Pakistan for further arms training. Salahuddin asked them to work for HM and advised them to go to Pakistan through the normal official channel and gave him an introductory letter addressed to Gulam Mohammad Safi of Muzaffarabad (in PoK) for helping him to join a training camp.

In August 1992, Asif tried to procure visitor visa from the Pakistan High Commission, in New Delhi. His request was turned down, as he failed to produce any sponsorship letter from Pakistan. After the demolition of Babri Masjid on 6 December 1992 and subsequent riots all over India, Asif's resolve to go to Pakistan strengthened. In January 1993, he along with 200 other Tablighi Jamaat activists went to Bangladesh and tried to get entry into Pakistan from there, but failed yet again. He went again to Kashmir the same year and met Salahuddin.

Salahuddin gauged Asif's eagerness and introduced

him to a doctor named Junaid (different from the Junaid of Azamgarh of Atif's module). Junaid was responsible for passing on instructions to Asif for carrying out terrorist activities in the rest of the country. Asif was tasked with targeting political leaders and economic targets such as markets, stock exchange, etc., in Kolkata. It was decided that Asif would take responsibility in the name of Minorities United Front (MUF) after successful terror activities by his group. Junaid was also tasked with arranging weapons for Asif's group. Thereafter, Asif returned to Kolkata. In 1994, Junaid asked them to collect arms and ammunitions from Delhi. However, they could not take the delivery as Asif was arrested by the Delhi Police in a TADA case and was subsequently lodged in Tihar Jail. Thus, all of Asif's attempts to go to Pakistan failed. He was now cooling his heels in jail.

In Tihar, he developed a strong bond with two inmates: Aftab Ansari, a criminal having a network of kidnappers and Ahmed Omar Saeed Sheikh, a known terrorist and London School of Economics (LSE) dropout. Omar had come to India to get some of the important terrorists in his outfit, Harkat-ul-Ansar (HuA), released from jail. HuA was a breakaway group of HuJI. It was formed under Fazlur Rehman Khalil for operations in Afghanistan and Kashmir. Within the first few months of its formation, HuA was able to train several thousand militants in J&K. When it was banned by the US in 1997, HuA morphed itself as Harkat-ul-Mujahideen (HuM).

After HuA's several unsuccessful attempts to get these important members out of jail, they sent Omar to India in 1994. He was tasked with kidnapping foreign nationals in India and making a trade for the terrorists lodged in Indian jails. He befriended four foreign tourists (three British and one American) in Delhi. He disguised himself as Rohit Sharma and concocted a story that his father had left behind a huge property in a village for him. He fascinated the foreigners with stories of rural and unseen India and persuaded them to visit his village. The Britons went willingly with him to his village in Saharanpur (UP), where as per the plan, they were held captive. The American was kept captive in Ghaziabad. HuA then demanded the government to release 10 of its militants in exchange for the captives.

However, Omar's plan went haywire when a police party of Ghaziabad, while investigating a theft case, chanced upon his hideout, where the American national was held captive. The hostage was freed in a dramatic rescue operation where Omar fired several shots at the police. He was subsequently overpowered, hit by a bullet and arrested along with a few members of his gang. On 1 November 1994, one of Omar's men led the policemen to the place where the three British nationals were held. A shoot-out ensued between the terrorists and the police, and a militant and two policemen were killed. Unfortunately, a few militants managed to escape in the melee.

Omar was kept in Tihar Jail, where he met Asif. But there was one more person who was no less important to Asif in achieving his deep desire of pursuing terror activities. He was Aftab Ansari.

Aftab Ansari was born in Varanasi in 1968. He completed his graduation in psychology from the Banaras Hindu University (BHU) in 1990. He then took admission in LLB in the same university. However, he dropped out after the first year. His elder brother, Anwar Ahmad Ansari, completed his graduation in journalism and LLB. Anwar started his career as an advocate, but soon went to the other side of law. He was arrested in Delhi for engaging in credit card frauds. While in Tihar, Anwar met the notorious kidnapper Dinesh Thakur, who was also lodged there. Dinesh and Aftab grew close through Anwar. Dinesh, after his release from jail, started visiting Aftab and asked him to join his kidnapping and extortion gang.

In 1995, Dinesh attempted to extort ₹5 lakh from a Delhi-based businessman. I was the DCP of North-West district in Delhi at that time. When the businessman approached me for help, I deputed Ravi Shankar to apprehend Dinesh. As per our plan, the businessman was instructed to continue negotiating with the kidnapper and, finally, a deal was struck. He agreed to pay ₹2 lakh to Dinesh in the Ashok Vihar market. A trap was laid by Ravi's team. When Dinesh showed up, the team tried to apprehend him, which resulted in an exchange of fire. I, too, rushed to the market and found an associate of Dinesh trying to make an escape. I, along with a constable, chased him down and nabbed him. Initially, he acted as a media person named Rajat Sharma, but on frisking, a weapon was recovered. He was brought to the police station, wherein he revealed his real identity as Aftab Ansari. While Dinesh died in the encounter, Aftab was arrested and sent to Tihar Jail. That is how Asif, Omar and Aftab met each other in Tihar and formed a close criminal–terror nexus.

Aftab was released from jail in November 1998 and he formed his own extortion gang. They kidnapped Anand Aggarwal, a coal merchant of Banaras, by impersonating as CBI officers and extorted ₹1.5 crore.

Meanwhile, on 24 December 1999, the extremist forces dealt a huge blow to the security through the hijacking of IC-814, an Indian Airlines flight, by HuM. The Government of India was forced to release Omar, Mushtaq Ahmed Zargar (alias Latram) and Mohammad Masood Azhar, a radical Islamist scholar from prison in exchange for the inflight passengers. Masood Azhar after reaching Pakistan, formed Jaish-e-Mohammed (JeM), a terrorist organization. Initially, Omar also joined JeM. Later, he started working with Al-Qaeda, LeT and HuJI.

Meanwhile, Asif had also been released from jail in August 1999 and Aftab called him to Lucknow. Both discussed their future plan of action and decided to create their own set-up of jihadis. To fund their terror activities, they planned to resort to kidnappings. Aftab contacted Omar for his help in sending people from India, via Bangladesh or Saudi Arabia, to Pakistan in Lashkar camps for training. Omar readily agreed.

Aftab told Asif that they should get counterfeit passports made. Asif reached out to his contact in the passport office in Patna and got a passport made in the name of Danish Hussain for himself. Aftab's fake name in the passport was Farhan Malik. Aftab shifted to Dubai. Asif remained in India and took part in kidnappings, splitting the ransom with Aftab. This arrangement worked fine for them. Their targets were rich businessmen in Mumbai, Delhi, Kolkata and other cities, from whom they extorted a substantial amount of money. Once successful in metro cities, they expanded their operations in other parts of India, too. Once, they received a ransom of ₹2.75 crore when they kidnapped a jeweler in Gujarat called Bhaskar Parikh.

They built a system to keep at arm's length during kidnappings, dividing the work amongst different teams, thus making it difficult for the police to track them. One team would decide the target, the actual kidnapping was done by a second team, the kidnapped was held in captivity by the third team while the negotiation would be done from abroad by the fourth team. Aftab and Asif would know the members of all the teams, but members of one team would not know the members of the other teams. As a result, even if any member of a team is caught by the police, he would not be able to reveal the identity of the other team members. Asif was heading the first team. Aftab himself was heading the fourth team and would negotiate the quantum of ransom with the family members of the kidnapped. He would do this while himself being located in Dubai. The ransom amount would be delivered to Aftab in Dubai through hawala, the kidnapped person would then be released.

Over time, Aftab's group raised enough money to manage their own terror outfit. Next, they needed a supply of arms and ammunition, and an arrangement for terror training. While in Dubai, Aftab had visited Omar in Pakistan many times. Many Pakistan-based terror outfits were in need of logistical support in India for establishing their own terror network. Thus, Aftab and Omar explored synergies to help each other out. These outfits took lessons from the LeT, which had established a well-knit terror network in India by 1995 with the help of a person called Syed Abdul Karim, alias Tunda. But how was the LeT able to establish such a network in India?

After the demolition of Babri Masjid in 1992, Tunda, who hailed from the Pilukhua area in UP, formed a group of youths who were angry by the turn of events in Ayodhya in particular and in the country in general. He joined hands with one Dr Jalees Ansari, who was known as Doctor Bomb. Tunda was also an expert in making bombs and it is said that he lost his hand while at his 'craft' and, hence, he came to be known with the nickname Tunda. In 1993, this group indulged in bomb blasts in trains in and around Mumbai. The CBI cracked these cases and Dr Ansari and others were arrested. Tunda, however, escaped to Pakistan, where he joined the LeT. He started delivering lectures in madarsas in Pakistan and Bangladesh, wherein he would spot potential recruits to radicalize for this cause. He also imparted training for the preparation of bombs in the LeT training camps. The LeT, with the help of Tunda, initially sent five trained terrorists to India to be settled as resident agents. Through his contacts, he helped them settle in Delhi, Hyderabad, Mumbai, Kolkata and Malerkotla (in Punjab). They all created fake Indian IDs and started working in their respective places. Their job was to indoctrinate more and more such youths who were angry and disenchanted with the alleged minority persecution. Once they were settled, more terrorists were sent by the LeT to aid these resident agents. Azam Cheema, who was the launching commander[36] of the LeT, and Tunda provided them support and direction. In 1996–97, this group caused more than 42 explosions all over India. At that time, I was working as DCP in the Crime Branch of the Delhi Police. Alok and Ravi were both working with me. My team cracked all of these blast cases, which resulted in the arrest of 27 LeT modules from all over India in 1998. It was a huge setback to the LeT.

The LeT was, however, relentless in its nefarious designs. Along with other terror groups in Pakistan, it found an opportunity in the form of Aftab and Asif, who could help them settle resident agents in India. Aftab planned a meeting with the terror outfits in December 2000 and asked Asif to reach Pakistan. Meanwhile, the LeT had already agreed to impart training to Aftab's group. The first sets of persons were sent from India in November 2000 to receive terror trainings in Pakistan.

Amongst the youths who were sent to Pakistan for these training camps was one Mohamed Sadique Israr, alias Sadakat. He belonged to Azamgarh, but his childhood was spent in Mumbai. He joined SIMI in 1996 and used to attend its weekly meetings in Mumbai. Through a relative, he met Asif in April

---

[36]One who sends trained terrorists for actual operations, provides them with logistics and assigns tasks.

2000. Asif invited him to Kolkata in July 2000. There, he met Aftab as well. Aftab organized training for him in Pakistan. Sadique reached Karachi along with five Indian Bengali men. They were given a 21-day combat training (Daura-e-Aam) in the Muzaffarabad (PoK) area. Thereafter, they were taken to a desert area for three months of specialized training (Daura-e-Khas). After the completion of his training, Sadique stayed in Bahawalpur (LeT accommodation), while five others left for India via Bangladesh.

Asif also reached Pakistan and met Mahfooz, who was in Tihar Jail with Asif and Aftab. He had returned to Pakistan on completion of his jail term in India. Aftab and Asif met Azam, the launching commander of LeT, who showed them the training camps of LeT located in PoK and Bahawalpur. Omar took them to a training centre in Afghanistan.

Aftab and Asif had a meeting with Azam and Tunda (LeT), Mehtab Mufti Kifayatullah and Mehboob (HuJI) and Omar (JeM, who later switched over to LeT and HuJI). Aftab assured financial and logistical assistance to them and offered his help in settling resident agents in India. In return, these outfits would supply arms and ammunition to them and provide training to their members.

The coming together of these devious minds was an indication of a ticking bomb, waiting to explode.

In March 2001, Aftab married the sister of Tahir Kashmiri, who had been in Tihar Jail with him and had settled in Pakistan along with his family after his release. Sadique and Asif attended the wedding. Aftab bought a house in Rawalpindi and another one in Dubai. His role was to coordinate with outfits in Pakistan. Asif came back to India and made Mumbai his base with his younger brother, Amir Raza Khan, to coordinate and command the terror activities in India. Sadique also returned to India via

Nepal. Aftab sent another set of trainees including Babu Bhai to a LeT camp in March–April 2001. Babu Bhai completed his training and returned to India in two months' time.

Simultaneously, the LeT and HuJI started sending their agents to India via Bangladesh. HuJI militants were sent by Omar, while LeT militants were sent by Azam. Before dispatching them to India, they were given extensive training of arms and ammunition, handling of computers, the internet and email for communications. They were cautioned not to use a telephone and to use only email to communicate with each other. They were briefed that each of them would enter India via Bangladesh one by one and establish themselves in big cities, such as Kolkata, Mumbai, Delhi, etc. They were told to get acquainted with the cultural norms and local dialects to effectively blend in as a resident agent. Once they were settled, tasks would be assigned to them. They were also taught code words for communication. 'Kapre' meant weapons. Mention of 'suit' referred to a single weapon. 'Pen/pencils' meant cartridges or rounds, 'anar' meant bomb, 'mithai/halwa' was used for explosives or RDX. 'Market' was used for India, while 'dukaan' was used for Pakistan and 'karkhana' for Bangladesh. Other code words included:

Faloos (Arabic word for 'money') – money

Karigar (artisan) – militant or associate

Mehman khana (guest house) – jail or arrest

Farishte (angels) – intelligence

Khatmal (bedbugs) – police

Musafir khana (inn) – Delhi

Pagal khana (mental asylum) – Agra

Karobar kar li hai (Business started or done) – Successfully established themselves as resident agents

Karobar band kar raha hun (Closing business) – Returning to Pakistan

Karobar badal raha hun (Changing business) – Shifting location/place/city

These resident agents started pouring into India through Bangladesh. Asif and Amir would help them settle in an Indian city. For example, in early 2001, Omar sent a terrorist named Arshad to Kolkata via Bangladesh for establishing him as a resident agent in Agra. Amir created the documents to establish that Arshad had an Indian identity, a driving licence and a ration card with a photograph of Arshad. Documents for Arshad were made in the name of Aslam Khan, showing him as a resident of West Bengal. He was given ₹40,000 before he set out for Agra. Arshad settled in Agra with the undercover of a businessman dealing in shoes, in the name of Marito Shoes. His identity as a resident of West Bengal helped in people in Agra easily accepting him to be of Indian origin.

By May 2001, HuJI and LeT were able to settle resident agents at various parts of the country: Nawab and Sunny in Delhi, Dilshad in Meerut (UP), Mufti Asrar in Saharanpur (UP), Inamul Haq in Gujarat, Munshi Asad in Gujarat, Arshad Khan in Agra, Wazid and Salim in Hazaribagh (Jharkhand), and Gulam Qadir Bhatt and Gulam Mohammad Dar in J&K.

Aftab then started sending consignments of weapons for the LeT/HuJI terrorists and for his own group. The first consignment containing five pistols was sent in March 2001, while the second containing five AK-47s and five pistols was sent in June 2001. The third consignment containing AK-47s, ammunition and RDX was also received by Asif.

On 25 July 2001, to raise more funds for their work, Asif kidnapped Partha Pratim Roy Burman of Khadim Shoes, Kolkata. Sadique, Babu Bhai and Arshad took part in the kidnapping. Aftab negotiated the ransom from Dubai and settled it at ₹5 crore. Partha was released after ₹3.75 crore was delivered to Aftab. Omar demanded an amount of US$1 lakh from Aftab from this extortion money as a donation to his terror outfit. Aftab, after consultation with Asif, gave the donation to Omar. Asif later read in a newspaper that Omar had delivered the same amount to Mohammed Atta, who was the main suspect in the ghastly 9/11 World Trade Center attack in the US.

While Aftab and the LeT/HuJI were active in enhancing their prowess to operate in various parts of the country, the intelligence agencies and police got wind of their activities. A Delhi Police team led by Ravi got information that a group based in Agra was planning a terror attack. His team followed the leads and located Arshad in Agra. This led to the arrest of Arshad and Asif. Based on their interrogation, the team tried to apprehend Amir from Mumbai. However, by that time he had fled to Dubai. Subsequently, Asif died in an encounter with the Gujarat Police on 7 December 2001.

Asif's death provoked Amir and Aftab to take revenge. On 22 January 2002, Aftab sent his teams located at Kolkata and Hazaribagh (it included Sadique and other terrorists of Pakistani origin) to carry out an attack at the American Center in Kolkata, which resulted in the death of four policemen and a security guard. Several civilians were also injured. Aftab claimed responsibility in the name of Asif Raza Commando Force. The Delhi Police got the leads and immediately sent a team led by Ravi Shankar to Hazaribagh to apprehend the suspects. What followed was a fierce encounter in which

Pakistani terrorist Mohammad Idris and Mohammad Salim were killed. With the help of the Interpol and the Federal Bureau of Investigation (FBI), Aftab was tracked down in Dubai and subsequently deported to India. Terrorists settled by LeT and HuJI were on the run, many of them returned to Pakistan and many others were arrested. Aftab terror group seemed to be collapsing. So how did they resurface and what was their relation to IM?

11

CONNECTING THE DOTS

Agni shesham rinah shesham shatruh shesham tathaiva cha
Punah punah pravardeth tasmaat shesham na kaarayet

(Fire, Loan and Enemy, if left even in small traces, will grow again and again; so it is advised to neutralize them completely.)

—Chanakya Neeti

Traces of Aftab's terror module reignited themselves to form another formidable group. Amir, after the arrest of his brother Asif, shifted to Dubai. He took over the reins of the Aftab-Asif terror module. He didn't have control over Aftab's gang of kidnappers and, thus, was not in a position to generate funds for terror operations. His requirements of support from the ISI/LeT/HuJI were far greater than those of Aftab, as Aftab was able to generate terror financing through his gang of kidnappers. Amir started rebuilding his contacts with ISI/LeT/ HuJI to garner support for training, funding and the supply of arms and ammunition and explosives.

The world was no longer the same post 9/11. Terror outfits across the globe started to face the heat of the respective countries where they were being instigated. Suddenly, the world view on terrorism changed leading to a robust consensus and partnerships in counterterrorism. Countries across the world became unanimous in taking strong action against terrorists and their financing. The UN and the Financial Action Task Force (FATF) made changes in their strategies to demolish terrorism effectively. The UN and FATF mandated nations not to tolerate terror financing or any other kind of support to the terror outfits in their jurisdictions. The ISI-sponsored terror outfits located in Pakistan were now reluctant in being directly involved in terror activities in India. They needed to realign their approach towards India with the new global reality. They needed a buffer that would keep them at a safe distance from India, without compromising on their terror activities. Amir became a safe bet for them and a symbiotic relationship developed between Amir and terror modules from across the border. Amir wanted to reunite the splintered group to increase its strength. He tried to locate its members by sending them emails since he was not in contact with any of them on phone. He also approached Qamar, who was the head of HuJI in Bangladesh and an associate of Aftab, to locate the scattered members. Two brothers, Riyaz Bhatkal and Iqbal Bhatkal, responded to Amir's call-out. They were not on police's radar and maintained a low profile. Amir called Riyaz to Dubai.

Sadique remained in hiding in Azamgarh for two months and then left for Mumbai. He responded to Amir's email who asked him to come to Dubai. Sometime in June or July 2002, Sadique reached Dubai, where he met Amir and Riyaz. Amir was setting up a shop named Yahya Electronics Shop. They discussed how to materialize their plan. Amir instructed Sadique and Riyaz to add new young Indian brigade in their militant group. Riyaz immediately returned to India, while

Sadique remained in Dubai for the next seven to eight months. After Dubai, Sadique reached Azamgarh and started his indoctrination programme. By the time he went back to Dubai to resume working in Amir's shop, he was able to radicalize Arif Badar and Dr Shahnawaz. They, in turn, were on the look-out for more such youths to bring into their fold. Meanwhile, Dr Shahnawaz and Rashid (a person radicalized by Arif) were sent for training to Pakistan via Dubai. After completing their training, the duo returned to India via Dubai and Nepal. Arif then sent Majid for training through the Dubai route.

In 2003, Babu Bhai received a message from Qamar, head of HuJI in Bangladesh, to meet him in Bangladesh. There, he met Amir and Qamar. Amir told him that their plan was to start terror activities in India through Bangladesh. Babu Bhai was tasked with recruiting members for training and escorting them between India and Bangladesh. Amir also asked him to recruit carriers to transport explosives from Bangladesh to India. Many people with allegiance to Amir as well as to HuJI were transported for training to Pakistan via Bangladesh and their return to India. Babu Bhai was managing all this.

At the other end, in Dubai, Amir told Sadique that he was 'closing down shop', as it was running into losses. Sadique thereafter returned to India by the end of 2003. Sadique, along with Arif, radicalized Atif Ameen and Sharfuddin (both from Azamgarh) and they were sent for training via Bangladesh through Babu Bhai in the middle of 2004.

The profiles of HuJI members in India and the members of IM exhibited a clear distinction. While the members of HuJI were mostly madrasa-educated, the members of IM had received their education in schools and colleges. This was perhaps due to the difference in the profiles of the leaders of the two groups. The leaders of HuJI in Bangladesh had a stronger connection with madrasa education and so they (and Babu Bhai) were more comfortable in reaching out to and radicalizing people from madrasas. On the other hand, Aftab, Atif and Riyaz, among others, had studied in mainstream educational institutes such as BHU, Jamia Millia, etc., and therefore, they were able to radicalize youth with similar educational backgrounds.

Atif had understood the need to form a larger group and, therefore, he prepared a scheme to motivate more people to join in. (It can't be said with absolute certainty whether this was his brainchild or if it was prepared by Amir or Riyaz or whether it was prepared by all of them together in consultation with each other.) The materials used for motivation was found in the electronic records seized from Batla House. They worked in the following order.

The indoctrination would start with a general discussion on religion: the Holy Quran and its interpretation and teachings of Hadiths. Atif would then start teaching how to do *wazoo* (cleansing the hands, legs and body before offering namaz) and offer namaz etc., in the correct way.

He would discuss the meaning and purpose of life and the role of jihad. Life after death, which was regarded as the real life, was then brought into discussion. Atif would explain that 'the life after death is a state of non-dying, that it was permanent and one gets result of one's action in that life, but this after-death life can be full of pleasure and luxury if one devotes himself in jihad in this life.[37]' He would further explain that 'a jihadi is also offered 72 *hoorein* (beautiful women) in that afterlife, that one can also receive *jannat* (heaven) for his parents.' They were told that doing jihad just once in their

---

[37]Here, the term 'jihad', which actually signifies an internal spiritual struggle, was misinterpreted by the proselytizer.

life was more beneficial than offering water to all hajis[38] and offering namaz or *roza* throughout one's life. According to him, jihad was not a new phenomenon. It had been there since ages against the disbelievers, the kafirs, and should be continued.

Besides his lectures on jihad, Atif would also talk on the injustice done against the Muslim community all over the world, particularly in Palestine, Iraq, Afghanistan and India (with special emphasis on J&K). He spoke of the 2002 Gujarat riots and the Mumbai riots after the demolition of Babri Masjid. He would show them photos and clippings of the Godhra incident in Gujarat, the Israeli–Palestinian conflict, alleged atrocities committed by the US in Iraq and alleged atrocities on Muslims in J&K.

He would give them various books downloaded from the internet to read. They included *Maidan Pukarate Hain* (about the Soviet–Afghan War); *Salah ad-Din Ayuubi* (on winning the war of Jerusalem); *Milestones*, Osama Bin Laden's biography, written by Sayyid Qutb; the English magazine *Combat* containing the photographs of charred dead bodies of Muslims; a book about the attack of US forces on Afghanistan and alleged atrocities committed by the US on Muslims, especially on women and children; and another one on alleged atrocities done on Iraqi Muslims by the US.

The reading list also included an untitled book on jihad, the gist of which was:

If there is any Muslim women in the custody of non-Muslim, or any land which was earlier ruled by Muslim but is now in the custody of a non-Muslim, and it comes into knowledge of any Muslim, then it becomes his right to conduct jihad

[38]A muslim who has been to Mecca as a pilgrim.

against such entity. If that Muslim after this knowledge does not fight, he should be slaughtered.

He also had a PowerPoint presentation with photographs of alleged atrocities done against Muslims in India and abroad. Videos containing visuals of alleged atrocities inflicted against Muslims were repeatedly played along with motivational songs calling all to join jihad.

One of the first persons radicalized by Atif and Sadique was Mohamad Saif, younger brother of Dr Shahnawaz. Next, Atif reached out to his childhood friends who were studying at various places but were close to him, people he could trust with his plans. The chain of radicalizing youths began and now some older members, too, joined in this endeavour. This group, known as the Azamgarh module of IM, started gaining strength now.

This group was now ready to launch its first operation and Varanasi was its first target. 23 February 2005 proved to be a deadly date for one of the oldest cities of Hindu civilization. Atif Amin and Shanawaz planted an explosive device at Dashashwamedha Ghat. It exploded at around 4.00 p.m., resulting in the death of seven persons and injuries to nine. They struck again in Varanasi on 7 March 2006. Sankat Mochan Mandir and the cantonment railway station were rocked by two powerful explosions that killed 28 people and injured more than 100. Sadique participated in planning and preparation of bombs, but didn't go for the actual operation. After the success of this operation, Atif started interacting with Amir directly and, therefore, Sadique decided to let Atif lead the Azamgarh module and he himself shifted to Mumbai. Sadique provided planning and support to Atif from Mumbai.

Their next target was Gorakhpur (UP) where Atif's group

executed explosions on 22 May 2006. The success of Atif's module depended on logistical support from HuJI, which had established its network in India through Babu Bhai, who was known both to Qamar and Amir. Amir used this network to send explosives, and arms and ammunitions to its modules, and to transport its members from India to Pakistan via Bangladesh for training and back.

Though Atif was getting supply of explosives from HuJI through Babu Bhai, he was himself arranging detonators and timers. The Bijnor (UP) module of HuJI in India was in need of detonators and timers and, therefore, at the instructions of Qamar, Babu Bhai came to meet Rocky/Guru, alias Atif, in Lucknow. Intelligence agencies got wind of the movements of Babu Bhai, which led to his arrest by the UP Police. However, Atif could not be arrested, as Babu Bhai was unable to give any lead about the whereabouts or real identity of Atif as he knew Atif by the name of Guru/Rocky. (Ariz Khan, alias Junaid, who was caught by the Special Cell in 2018, revealed during his interrogation that Guru was none other than Atif. Finally, the mystery of Guru also came to a conclusive end.)

Babu Bhai's arrest was a major blow to HuJI's and Amir's modules, as it choked the supply and transportation of explosive materials to Atif. Atif then turned to Amir for the supply of explosives.

Another module of Amir's group was reverberating in Pune (the Pune module). It was headed by the Bhatkal brothers—Iqbal and Riyaz (Iqbal being the elder one). Riyaz had taken training in Pakistan in 2002–03, through Amir. It is not known if Iqbal had also undergone training. Both the brothers were deeply religious. They started radicalizing educated youths from Bhatkal (Karnataka) and Pune. In 2004, Iqbal formed a small group in Bhatkal called Usaba, consisting of 13 people. Usaba members met regularly, mostly on Fridays at Iqbal's house. They discussed issues such as finances, logistics, procurement of explosive materials, recruiting new talent and spirituality. Camps were organized in Bhatkal to motivate more people. At the end of 2005, one of its members, Yasin Bhatkal, was sent to Pakistan for training with the help of Amir. Amir met Yasin in Pakistan and gave him his email ID, but Riyaz instructed him not to interact with Amir directly. He was given extensive training in handling of weapons and making bombs using different types of explosives.

Riyaz wanted to get a website made for his terror outfit, i.e., IM. He engaged Mansoor, alias Peerbhoy (an expert in computers) in March 2007 for this purpose. Riyaz asked him to make the website so that they could proclaim their mission on it. However, Peerbhoy advised him against it, as the police could easily trace the IP address from which the website was created. Therefore, that plan was abandoned and instead Riyaz sent Peerbhoy for a course on ethical hacking from E2 Labs in Hyderabad in May 2007.

When Yasin returned from his training in Pakistan, he was tasked with preparing bombs for both the modules (Azamgarh and Pune). The required explosive materials were arranged by Riyaz. The first target of the Pune module was Hyderabad, wherein simultaneous explosions were caused in Lumbini Amusement Park and Gokul Chat Bhandar (two more bombs were defused from other parts of the city) on 25 August 2007.

After getting explosive materials from the Pune module, the Azamgarh module caused serial explosions in UP courts at Varanasi, Faizabad and Lucknow on 23 November 2007. This was the first instance when this group sent an email in the name of Indian Mujahideen claiming responsibility for these blasts. The email was sent five minutes before the explosions took place, making it evident that this email was *not* a prank. Till then, the name 'Indian Mujahideen' was unknown.

It is not clear why this email was sent. Was it on the instructions of the ISI or LeT? Did Amir himself decide to send this email? Was it decided by Riyaz, or was it a collective decision of both the modules? Were they audacious and proud? Were they challenging the investigating agencies?

Meanwhile, Yasin made a hideout in a three-acre farm at Kuppa in Udupi (Karnataka). The farm was taken on lease by one of the group members. It was suitable for preparation of bombs and for imparting training. In November 2007, Yasin imparted training to some of the members of the Pune module on the instructions of Riyaz.

Amir decided that the time had come to unleash terror in Gujarat. He asked Atif and Riyaz to work together on the plan. Surat and Ahmedabad were chosen as the targets. Riyaz and Iqbal started planning for terror action in Gujarat around March–April 2008. They asked Yasin to prepare around 100 boat-shaped/C-shaped bombs. While Yasin was in the process of preparing bombs for Gujarat, Riyaz asked for 10 bombs, which Yasin delivered to him on 5 May 2008. Riyaz, in turn, got them delivered to Atif's module.

Atif's group then struck at Jaipur on 13 May 2008. This time, the email was sent on 14 May to the media under the name of IM from a cybercafé in Sahibabad, UP. Since IM had adopted this practice of sending emails just before a blast, the surveillance and subsequent investigation on cybercafés were increased drastically. This unnerved Atif and he consulted Riyaz if there was another safe method to send emails. Riyaz, in turn, asked the tech-savvy Peerbhoy if it was possible to send an email without being detected. Peerbhoy was an expert in decoding Wi-Fi techniques and he assured Riyaz that he could send such an email without getting detected. Riyaz told him that the time for blasts in Gujarat was approaching, so he would be asked to send an email to the electronic and print media on behalf of IM. Peerbhoy came up with an idea. As per the plan, the wireless networks located in Pune were not to be used to send these emails. Instead, the emails would be sent from a Wi-Fi address in Mumbai, so that the police could not discover that they were staying in Pune. Peerbhoy and his team took a round of Mumbai and identified some open Wi-Fi connections that could be used. The contents of the email were dictated to Peerbhoy by Iqbal between 20 and 25 July 2008.

Meanwhile, SIMI (the Safdar Nagori faction) had started radicalizing its cadre and organized training camps in various parts of the country. SIMI was looking for outside support for violent action. In March 2008, the central government took strong action against SIMI and many members of the Safdar Nagori faction, including Nagori were arrested. After the arrest of Safdar, Subhan Qureshi (alias Tauqeer) and Qayamuddin Kapadia of Gujarat were elevated to the leadership role.

Abdul Subhan Qureshi, born in 1971, hailed from Moradabad, but his childhood was spent in Mumbai. He completed his graduation in industrial engineering and also did some computer courses. He started participating in SIMI's activities in 1990. Qayamuddin Kapadia, born in 1982, hailed from Vadodara and had studied up to Class 12. He joined SIMI in 2003.

SIMI had organized many training camps, but they didn't have any expertise in imparting training in the handling of explosive devices. Safdar Nagori had time and again mentioned in SIMI's training camps that he would contact Al-Qaeda/LeT for support. After Nagori's arrest, Subhan and Qayamuddin were trying to find a connection to these outfits. Subhan and

Riyaz knew each other well since 1995 when both of them used to attend meetings of SIMI in Kurla (Mumbai). When Riyaz needed logistical support in Gujarat, he sought support from Subhan somewhere in May–June in 2008. Subhan, in turn, asked Qayamuddin (as he was from Gujarat), to arrange the support needed by Riyaz. Qayamuddin got in touch with Riyaz and Atif, and promised to provide accommodation and manpower.

Meanwhile, Yasin had prepared the boat-shaped structures required for planting bombs at Surat and Ahmedabad. Riyaz asked one of his associates to prepare electronic timers. He designed and prepared printed circuit boards (PCBs) and got them manufactured and supplied to Riyaz. Riyaz got electronic items mounted on these PCBs. Since PCBs were not sufficient in number, Riyaz decided to use Quartz clocks as timers in Ahmedabad and PCBs in Surat.

The logistical support in Gujarat was provided by SIMI. Prior to the Gujarat attack, the modus operandi of the IM group was to extensively recce the targeted places during daytime and return to base by night. They prepared bombs at the base and then travelled to the targeted place on the scheduled day to plant the bombs and returned to base. They would not take any local support for either selection of target or for accommodation.

This was the first time that the Pune and Azamgarh modules stayed in accommodations provided by local SIMI activists. This departure from their well-established modus operandi of not involving outsiders in their operation proved fatal as the Gujarat Police got information on these accommodations and arrested the SIMI activists. However, two important SIMI leaders (Qayamuddin and Subhan), who had actually liaised with IM, could not be caught at that time, which thwarted the Gujarat Police's chance of tracing the IM modules.

The Pune module involved another outsider, a thief named Afzal Usmani, who was known to Riyaz. Before joining IM, Riyaz was involved in an extortion racket and Afzal had joined his criminal gang in 2002. Riyaz asked Afzal to arrange four vehicles for Gujarat. Afzal stole those vehicles from Navi Mumbai and delivered them at the accommodations in Gujarat.

After the 2008 Gujarat blasts, the Mumbai Police started picking up car thieves and interrogating them. In the process, Afzal was arrested on 27 August. Afzal proved to be a hard nut to crack and did not initially disclose anything about supplying vehicles in Gujarat.

Riyaz lapsed on one more count. Yasin had been successfully making bombs, and clock timers were used by IM since the beginning. However, Riyaz got the electronic timers etched on the PCBs, on which electronic items were mounted. The person who mounted the electronic items failed to mount one capacitor on these boards. The timers, therefore, failed resulting in the failure of IM's operation in Surat. Afzal had supplied four cars, two each for Ahmedabad and Surat. The cars used in Ahmedabad were destroyed as a result of the explosion of bombs planted in them, but the cars used in Surat were found intact. The investigation of the intact cars found in Surat led to the discovery that these vehicles were stolen from Navi Mumbai and that is how the Mumbai Police interrogated many car thieves including Azfal.

The Gujarat Police, on the other hand, was able to apprehend the SIMI group, which had provided local support to IM. The accused knew nothing about the real identity of the IM members and, hence, members of IM could not be identified. Undeterred by these arrests, Atif's module attacked Delhi on 13 September 2008. Bombs were prepared by Yasin and he delivered them to Mohamad Saif and Mohamad Khalid in Manipal. A mail was sent by Peerbhoy to the media about the blasts.

After the Delhi blasts, the Maharashtra Police again started interrogating car thieves including Afzal. This time, he cracked under pressure and confessed about his involvement in the Gujarat blasts. He also identified the houses where he had delivered the cars. He told the police that one Abu Bashir along with 12 of his associates had travelled to Delhi after planting the bombs. The investigation headed by Mohan based on this information, coupled with the three phone numbers that were used by IM during the Gujarat operation, had led the Special Cell to Batla House.

After the Batla House encounter, the IM modules of Pune and Azamgarh and some SIMI members involved in the Gujarat blasts were on the run. We were getting actionable intelligence inputs on their movements and anti-terror units of several state police were able to hunt them down. The Mumbai Police arrested 21 IM members. The Delhi Police arrested five while two died in an encounter. The UP Police arrested one. Yasin, Iqbal and Riyaz and one more of their associate, Mohsin Chaudhary, were on the run, moving together to avoid the police.

Yasin had one more place to escape to and that was Darbhanga in Bihar. In 2002, he had opened a perfumery and naturopathy medicines (unani) shop near Noor Masjid in Bhatkal. He was known by the name of Dr Imran of Unani Medicine among the college students. His perfume shop had attracted students of the Anjuman Engineering College, some of who hailed from Darbhanga. They would gather at his shop and amidst the aroma of perfumes and wisdom of ancient medicine, Islamic religious issues were discussed. In 2002, he sheltered a few boys from Darbhanga after they thrashed a local Shetty boy and the police was searching for them. That's when he grew close to the students from Darbhanga. The dispute was subsequently resolved due to the college's intervention. In November that year, he visited Darbhanga and stayed with those students. The bond between Yasin and Darbhanga became strong. Now, he was looking for a safe haven and his natural choice was Darbhanga. He contacted Qateel (from Darbhanga) and asked him to arrange accommodation for them.

In the first week of January 2009, four of them went to Darbhanga and stayed in a rented accommodation. The Darbhanga boys arranged a Nepali passport for Riyaz, Iqbal and their associate, Mohsin. They travelled to Nepal on those passports and subsequently went to Dubai from there. Iqbal settled in Dubai, while Riyaz went to Pakistan. Many of the other members of both the modules also went to Pakistan or Dubai.

However, Yasin had other plans. He was still on the path of jihad and was determined to continue terror activities. He started treating patients with his unani medicines in Darbhanga. Youths who visited his clinic were served other than unani herbs and medicines, a copious dose of radical and extremist ideas. He started to radicalize the youth there and in a short span of time became a popular therapist who could cure both the broken body and a tattered soul. Later, he shifted base to Delhi and stayed at Gohar Aziz Khomeini's house in the Shaheen Bagh area. Gohar also hailed from Darbhanga. He started working in the mechanical workshop in Mir Vihar. The workshop belonged to a person called Irshad, alias Chacha.

In June 2009, Riyaz contacted Yasin and nominated him to lead IM in India. He was promised financial help to increase jihadi activities and to recruit more youths. The Mumbai Police was after him in Pune and Bhatkal and as such, he couldn't go back there. He, however, had built a sizeable following in Darbhanga, which became his recruiting ground. His travels between Delhi and Darbhanga increased and the Darbhanga module was activated. He was also able to persuade the owner of the workshop, Irshad, to manufacture weapons, i.e., pistols and AK-47 rifles.

Riyaz came to know that Yasin needed weapons, so he struck a deal in Bangladesh to supply weapons to him. Yasin went to Kolkata to receive the consignment, but was arrested by the police in a theft case. He was able to hoodwink the police with a false name and came out of the prison within just 45 days.

The Darbangha module selected Pune as its target since they wanted to take revenge for the arrests of members of the Pune module. Riyaz got the explosives supplied through a person called Ibrahim (a member of Riyaz's group hailing from Bhatkal). They selected German Bakery and Shreemant Dagdusheth Halwai Ganpati Mandir as targets. On 13 February 2010, Yasin planted the bomb in German Bakery, but his associate, Qateel, failed to plant the bomb in the mandir. The German Bakery is situated in Koregaon Park, near the Jewish Chabad House and Osho International Meditation Resort. The bomb exploded at around 7.15 p.m. The famous bakery was reduced to rubbles. At the time of the blast, the place was bustling with students and foreign visitors. Seven people were killed and more than 60 were injured. It was one of the most gruesome attacks Pune had witnessed.

Yasin returned to Delhi and continued to design and manufacture weapons in the workshop. He also obtained a pistol and a carbine as samples from Munger in Bihar. He did extensive online research on weapon-manufacturing process and utilized his knowledge acquired during his training in

Pakistan. He was now able to produce about three carbines and five to six pistols in almost six months.

Emboldened by their Pune attack, Yasin and Riyaz planned their next target. They zeroed in on M. Chinnaswamy Stadium, in Bangalore, where an Indian Premier League (IPL) cricket match was to be played. Around 3.00 a.m. on 17 April, Yasin and his team planted five bombs at the main entry gates and ticket counters of the stadium. The match was to begin in a few hours' time and several thousands of spectators were expected. This was 2010 and by this time, the IPL franchise had caught the imagination of the cricket-crazy country.

As expected, the stadium was packed with spectators. An hour before the start of the match, two bombs exploded at the entry of the stadium. Fifteen people were injured. The other three bombs were defused by the police. By the time the bombs exploded, most of the spectators had already taken their seats in the stadium, and therefore, a major catastrophe was averted.

In July the same year, Riyaz sent a Pakistani national named Ajmal for taking part in terror activities in India. He came through Nepal and Yasin brought him to a hideout in Samastipur, Bihar. By the end of July, Yasin and Riyaz had decided to carry out an attack on Chabad House in Paharganj to target Jews. Yasin stole a black Passion motorcycle for this operation. On 1 August, Qateel and Ajmal were on their way on the motorcycle to attack Chabad House when Qateel's carbine went off accidently and he received a bullet injury in his hip. The operation was abandoned and Ajmal was sent back to Pakistan via Nepal. Riyaz then sent Danial (Asadullah Akhtar, alias Haddi, resident of Azamgarh, UP) and a Pakistani national Javed (alias Waqas).

The second anniversary of the Batla House encounter was approaching, and Yasin and Riyaz had plans. They wanted to avenge the encounter by attacking foreign tourists near Jama Masjid. The Commonwealth Games were due to begin the following month and targeting foreign tourists right before the games would attract international attention.

Explosives were purchased from Sadar Bazar in Delhi and a motorcycle and a car were stolen for the operation. As per the plan, two assailants were to fire at foreign tourists in and around the Jama Masjid area. This would attract media attention and the Jama Masjid police station would become the epicentre of all media queries. By that time, the car fitted with bombs and parked at the entry gate of the police station would explode. It would be timed to coincide with the gathering of media persons and additional police force to take byte. By attacking foreign tourists, the media and the police, IM wanted to send a strong signal. As per the plan, Javed and Danial reached Gate no. 3 of Jama Masjid and started firing at the tourists, injuring a couple of Taiwanese tourists. Yasin had left his house much before them in the stolen car, in which the bomb was fitted. He then parked this car in front of the Jama Masjid police station.

I was posted as Joint CP, Northern Range and as such Jama Masjid was under my jurisdiction. As soon I got the information that there had been a firing incident on foreigners, I left for Jama Masjid. While on my way, I got additional information that smoke was coming out of a suspicious car parked at the gate of the police station. On reaching the police station, I inspected the car with my team and found it to be fitted with an explosive device that had failed to explode. I realized that the vehicle at the gate was parked to target mainly police officers of the Range and the Special Cell, and the media who were expected to visit the crime scene. I thanked God that this attempt of the terrorists failed, else it would have resulted in the loss of many lives.

After the attack at the Jama Masjid area, Javed and Danial were shifted to Samastipur. Riyaz then asked Yasin to carry out an attack around the anniversary of Babri Masjid demolition. On 7 December 2010, they planted a bomb at Sheetla Ghat near Ashwamedha Ghat in Varanasi (UP). The explosion resulted in the death of an infant and injuries to 20 people.

In June 2011, Riyaz asked Yasin to plant bombs in Mumbai. They recced the city and on 13 July, planted bombs at Zaveri Bazar, Opera House and Dadar. Three explosions took place between 6.45 p.m. and 7.06 p.m., killing 17 and injuring 131.

Special Cell's Sanjeev, along with his team, had been working on IM since the Batla House encounter. His team developed intelligence on the Darbhanga module and between November and December 2011, arrested 11 of its members, thereby dismantling this module. During interrogation, Qateel revealed the name of its leader as Dr Imran Khan. When the photographs of the wanted persons of IM were shown, he identified Dr Imran as Yasin. Yasin was on the run and shifted to Nepal in February 2012. He was finally arrested on 29 August 2013 from the Indo-Nepal border and his arrest resulted in the neutralization of all the modules of IM in India.

After the Batla House encounter and the arrests by different state police, the top leaders of IM, namely Iqbal Bhatkal and Riyaz Bhatkal (from Karnataka); Mohsin Chaudhary (from Maharastra); Dr Shahnawaz, Abu Rashid and Mirza Shadab Beg (all from Azamgarh) escaped to Pakistan via Nepal after being on the run for several months in India. Iqbal later shifted to Dubai.

Are they still active and in the process of strengthening and creating new modules or are they spent force? Have they been neutralized? Nothing is known for sure. There are many stories floating in the intelligence world. One version is that the

Azamgarh module joined the Islamic State in Iraq and Syria (ISIS) and, in December 2014, it migrated to Syria, where they were killed. Another version is that Mirza Shadab Beg, who hails from Azamgarh, and some of his associates were killed in covert operations in Pakistan by Indian security agencies. Yet another version says that the Bhatkal brothers (Riyaz and Iqbal) have been missing for the past three to four years. Where are they? Are they still working or are they deadwood? Only time will tell.

EPILOGUE

The Batla House encounter was the beginning of the downfall of IM. During this decade, all the questions of the Batla House encounter and IM have been answered in different forums and courts of law. Many IM terrorists have been arrested and put to court trials in bomb blast cases.

The trials of several cases are still ongoing and progressing gradually. Two bomb blast cases have concluded to date, i.e., the Hyderabad serial blast case of 25 August 2007 and the Jaipur serial blast case of 13 May 2008. Both resulted in the conviction of the accused.

While most of the IM members have been arrested, some evaded arrest and took shelter at various places including Pakistan, Dubai and Nepal. The Special Cell was on the lookout for Shahzad Ahmed alias Pappu, and Ariz Khan alias Junaid, who had escaped from Flat no. 108, L-18, Batla House, on 19 September 2008.

Shahzad had taken shelter in his village, Mohalla Baz Bahadur (Kote Kila Road, Azamgarh) after his escape. He was arrested by the Anti-Terrorism Squad (ATS), UP Police, on 1 February 2010 from Khalispur village in Azamgarh. The Delhi Police Crime Branch, which was investigating the Batla House encounter case, took him on remand. During interrogation, he admitted that he was present at Flat no. 108, L-18, Batla House during the raid and encounter. He confirmed that he managed to escape along with Junaid while firing at the police team. This revelation aligned with the testimonies of the Special Cell team that two people had escaped from Batla House.

After completion of its investigation, the Delhi Police Crime Branch sent the case for trial in the court. The trial court convicted Shahzad on 25 July 2013, and on 30 July, sentenced him to life imprisonment for his involvement in the Batla House encounter. Shahzad has filed an appeal in the Delhi High Court.

Junaid had escaped to Nepal and occasionally visited India. The Delhi Police Special Cell had been trying to keep track of him. A team of the Special Cell working under DCP Pramod Kushwaha got the lead and arrested him on 13 February 2018 near Sharda Inter College, Banbasa, Indo-Nepal border. He was later taken on police remand by the Crime Branch in connection with the Batla House encounter. The Crime Branch has completed the investigation and has sent the case for trial and the decision is awaited.

The Batla House encounter became a historic event in the fight against terrorism. It caused a critical blow to IM, as it neutralized its key members and broke the backbone of its network in India. We lost one of the most intelligent and brave officers, whose findings led us to the core IM members. The work done by all the Special Cell personnel helped crack the bomb blast cases and neutralize the threat from this terror group that had caused many blasts across the country between 2004 and 2008, causing injuries to 765 people and killing 239 innocent men, women and children.

This case stirred a political storm, instigated a witch-hunt against Special Cell officers, divided public opinion and became a raging controversial topic in the media that continues till date. The aftermath of this incident brought to the fore many systemic issues that officers face while discharging their duties towards the country. There is a dire need for India to have a political consensus on how to deal with terrorism and to build a national policy on it.

ANNEXURE 1[1]

Alok Kumar, a DANIPS officer of 1985 batch and inducted into IPS in 2000, was posted in the Special Cell as DCP during the Batla House encounter. He is the recipient of a Police Medal for Gallantry (PMG), President's Police Medal for Meritorious Service, President's Police Medal for Distinguished Service and UN Medal for service with the United Nations Mission in Bosnia.

Alok Kumar, an IPS officers of 1996 batch, was the DCP of Central District.

Anil Tyagi, ASI (now SI), was part of Mohan Chand Sharma's 18-member team. He is the recipient of one PMG.

Balwant Singh, HC (now ASI), was part of the seven-member team that raided L-18, Batla House. He suffered bullet injury during the encounter. He is the recipient of one PMG, four Asadharan Karya Puruskars (AKP) and one out-of-turn promotion.

---

[1]The names of the officers who have been referred to in this book. These are in alphabetical order.
Some of the abbreviations used here are as follows.
PPMG: President's Police Medal for Gallantry,
PMG: Police Medal for Gallantry, and
AKP: Asadharan Karya Puruskar.

Birender Negi, constable (now HC), was part of Mohan's 18-member team. He is the recipient of one out-of-turn promotion, one PMG and two AKPs.

Chhanda Sahejwani, SI (now Inspector Technical), is an electronic and telecommunication engineer and was assisting the Special Cell as a technical supervisor.

Dalip Kumar, SI (now Inspector), was part of Mohan's 18-member team. He is the recipient of one PMG and one AKP.

Devender Singh, SI (now Inspector), was part of Mohan's 18-member team. He is the recipient of three out-of-turn promotions, one President's Police Medal for Gallantry (PPMG) and one PMG.

Dharmender Kumar, SI (now Inspector), was part of the seven-member team that entered Flat no. 108, L-18, Batla House. He was in the guise of a Vodaphone executive. He is the recipient of one out-of-turn promotion and two PMGs.

Gurmeet Singh, HC, took HC Balwant to the hospital after the latter sustained bullet injury. He is the recipient of one out-of-turn promotion, one PMG and three AKPs.

Manish Kumar, HC, was part of Mohan's 18-member team that raided Batla House. He is the recipient of one AKP.

Mohan Chand Sharma (martyr), inspector, an officer of the 1989 batch, led the first team to Flat no. 108, L-18, Batla House. He received bullet injuries during the encounter and later succumbed to those injuries. He was the recipient of two PPMGs (he was awarded a PPMG posthumously) and six PMGs. He was posthumously awarded the Ashoka Chakra for his gallant act in the Batla House encounter.

Rahul Kumar Singh, SI (now Inspector), was in the seven-member team that entered L-18, Batla House. He is the recipient of one out-of-turn promotion, three PMGs and one AKP.

Rajan Bhagat (DCP), an officer of 1981 batch, has worked in various capacities in the Delhi Police. He was the press relation officer of the Delhi Police during Batla House encounter.

Late Rajbir Singh, HC, entered L-18, Batla House with Sanjeev Yadav. During the encounter, Rajbir was hit by two bullets in his bullet-proof jacket. He was the recipient of one out-of-turn promotion, one PMG and one AKP.

Rajeev, constable (now ASI), was part of Mohan's 18-member team. He is the recipient of one out-of-turn promotion and one PMG.

Rakesh Malik, SI (now Inspector), was part of Mohan's 18-member team. He is the recipient of three out-of-turn promotions.

Ravi Shankar, ACP (retired as DCP), was part of the investigation team of the Special Cell. He was instrumental in solving the 42 blast cases of 1996–98. He is the recipient of two out-of-turn promotions, one PMG, President Police Medal for distinguish services and President Police Medal for Meritorious Services.

Ravinder Kumar Tyagi, SI (now Inspector), was part of the seven-member team that entered L-18, Batla House. He is the recipient of three PMGs, one President's Medal for distinguish services and three AKPs.

Sandeep Singh, constable (now HC), was part of Mohan's 18-member team. He is the recipient of one AKP.

Sanjay Dutt, inspector (now ACP), was part of Mohan's investigation team. He is the recipient of one out-of-turn promotion and two PMGs.

Sanjeev Kumar Yadav, DCP, an officer of the 1998 DANIPS batch, he led the backup team during the Batla House encounter. He is the recipient of one PPMG and eight PMGs.

Satender Singh, HC (now ASI), was part of Mohan's 18-member team. He is the recipient of one out-of-turn promotion and one PMG.

Satender Kumar, HC (now ASI), was part of the seven-member team that entered L-18, Batla House. He is the recipient of one out-of-turn promotion, one PMG and five AKPs.

Udaibir Singh, HC (now ASI), was part of the seven-member team that entered L-18, Batla House. He is the recipient of one out-of-turn promotion.

Vinod Gautam, HC (now ASI), was part of Mohan's 18-member team. He is the recipient of one out-of-turn promotion and one PMG.

ANNEXURE 2[2]

Abu Al Kama was the head of LeT in J&K, in 2005. He planned and executed the October 2005 blasts in Delhi. Later, he returned to Pakistan. He was monitoring and planning the activities of IM.

Abu Huzefa was the second-in-command of the LeT in J&K, in 2005. He took part in the planning and execution of the October 2005 blasts in Delhi. He later died in Kashmir during an encounter with the Special Cell of the Delhi Police.

Abu Rashid (Azamgargh module) went for training to Pakistan via Dubai. He shifted base to Pakistan after the Batla House encounter.

Abdul Subhan Qureshi, alias Tauqeer (SIMI), joined SIMI in 1990 and became the head of the Safdar Nagori faction after the arrest of Nagori. His group provided logistical support to IM during the Gujarat blasts.

Aftab Ansari (IM) is a criminal-turned-terrorist and the co-founder of IM. He caused the attack on the American Center in Kolkata on 22 January 2002. He has been convicted in this

---

[2]The names of the terrorists mentioned in the book.

case to be hanged till death. At present, he is in Kolkata Jail, pending his execution.

Afzal Mutalib Usmani, a criminal and car thief, had joined the extortion gang of Riyaz Bhatkal in 2002. He stole four vehicles from Navi Mumbai and delivered them in Gujarat to be used for the Gujarat blasts of July 2008.

Ahmed Omar Saeed Sheikh kidnapped four foreigners and demanded the release of 10 HuA militants. He, however, was arrested and the hostages were rescued. He was released in December 1999 after the hijacking of the Indian Airlines Flight 814, commonly known as IC 814. He helped Asif Raza Khan and Aftab Ansari in the formation of the terror group. He was later sentenced to death by a Pakistani court for the kidnapping and murder of the *Wall Street Journal* reporter Daniel Pearl.

Ajmal was a Pakistani terrorist sent by Riyaz Bhatkal in July 2010 to India for taking part in terror activities. He returned to Pakistan in August 2010.

Amir Raza Khan (IM), younger brother of Asif Raza Khan, worked in the shadow of Asif and Aftab Ansari. After the death of Asif and the arrest of Aftab, he took over the reins of IM.

Arif Badar (Azamgarh module) was an expert in bomb-making and radicalizing youths. He participated in the Ahmedabad and Jaipur blasts and prepared timers for bombs used in the Delhi blasts.

Ariz Khan, alias Junaid (Azamgarh module) was one of the terrorists who escaped from Flat no. 108, L-18 during the Batla

House encounter. He was later caught by the Special Cell of the Delhi Police in 2018. He participated in many blasts across the country.

Arshad Khan, a Pakistani terrorist having allegiance to HuJI, he was settled as a resident agent in Agra (UP) by IM. He, along with Asif, was arrested in 2001 by the Delhi Police.

Asadullah Akhtar, alias Haddi (Azamgarh module) alias Danial, returned to India in August 2010 after taking training in Pakistan. He took part in the Jama Masjid attack of 19 September 2010. He also planted bombs in Varanasi in 2006 and was part of the Delhi blasts, too.

Asif Raza Khan (IM) along with Aftab Ansari was the co-founder of IM. He was killed in a police encounter in December 2001.

Azam Cheema is the launching commander of the LeT. He attended meetings with Aftab and Asif in 2001 to finalize their plans to carry out terror activities in India.

Babu Bhai, alias Jalaluddin Molla, was an active member of HuJI and he had carried RDX from Bangladesh to different cities in India.

Dinesh Thakur was a kidnapper whose gang Aftab had joined. He was killed in an encounter with the Delhi Police in July 1995.

Dr Shahnawaz (Azamgarh module) is a Pakistani trained terrorist and was part of conspiracy in the Delhi blasts. After the Batla House encounter, he shifted to Pakistan.

Hafiz Naushad had established a module of HuJI in Bijnore (UP).

Hakim Mohd. (Azamgarh module) carried two bags of ball bearings from Lucknow to Delhi, which were used in the Delhi blasts.

Iqbal Bhatkal was heading the Pune module of IM. He caused blasts in Hyderabad in 2007, and planned and executed blasts in Gujarat in 2008. After the Batla House encounter, he shifted to Pakistan and Dubai and headed the Darbhanga module of IM.

Majid (Azamgarh module) was motivated by Arif Badar and took training in Pakistan.

Mansoor, alias Peerbhoy (Pune Module), was an expert in computers and the media head of IM. He sent three emails on behalf of IM, exploiting open Wi-Fi facilities in cybercafés. He was Principal Engineer in Zimbra, a subsidiary of Yahoo! Web Services India Pvt. Ltd, Pune.

Mohamad Khalid, alias Kodi (Azamgarh module), planted bombs in Jaipur, Ahmedabad and Delhi. He along with Mohamad Saif brought explosives from Manipal for the Delhi blasts.

Mohamad Saif (Azamgarh module) took part in all the blasts caused by the Azamgarh module. He was caught in L-18, Batla House, during the encounter.

Mohd. Atif Ameen, alias Guru (head of the Azamgarh module), was trained in Pakistan. He was killed in the Batla House encounter.

Mohd. Shakeel, alias Ajay (Azamgarh module), took part in causing explosions in Ahmedabad and Delhi.

Mirza Shadab Beg (Azamgarh module) participated in a number of blasts caused by IM. He fled to Pakistan after the Batla House encounter.

Mufti Bashir Abu (SIMI), was a resident of Azamgarh who gave speeches in the training camps arranged by Safdar Nagori. He used to exhort trainees to join jihad. He was arrested by the Gujarat Police in August 2008 due to his involvement in the Gujarat blasts of July 2008.

Qamar, alias Nata, was heading HuJI in Bangladesh. He worked closely with Aftab and Asif and later with Amir. He established his network in India with the help of IM.

Qayamuddin Kapadia (SIMI) provided logistical support to IM during the Gujarat blasts.

Riyaz Bhatkal (operational head of the Pune module) caused blasts in Hyderabad in 2007 and planned and executed the 2008 Gujarat blasts. After the Batla House encounter, he shifted to Pakistan and headed the Darbhanga module.

Sadique Israr, alias Sadakat (Azamgarh module), took training in LeT camps in Pakistan. He was part of the team that attacked the American Center in Kolkata in January 2002. He was arrested by the Mumbai Police in September 2008.

Safdar Nagori (SIMI hardliner) led the radical group after the split in SIMI on 10 April 2006. The Madhya Pradesh Police arrested him in March 2008.

Salman (Azamgarh module) planted bombs in Gorakhpur, Jaipur and Ahmedabad and was part of the conspiracy for Delhi blasts.

Sajid Mohd. alias Chhota Sajid alias Pankaj (Azamgarh module) died during the Batla House encounter. He took part in all the blasts carried out by the Azamgarh module.

Sajid Mohd., alias Sajid Bada (Azamgarh Module), planted bombs in Jaipur, Ahmedabad and Delhi.

Saqib Nissar (Azamgarh module) took part in recce for the Ahmedabad blasts and conspiracy in the Delhi blasts.

Shahbaz Hussain (SIMI) was arrested by the Rajasthan Police from Lucknow on 25 August 2008 for his involvement in the Jaipur blast of 13 May 2008.

Shahzad Ahmed, alias Pappu (Azamgarh module), planted a bomb in the children's park in New Delhi. He was one of the two persons who escaped from Flat no. 108, L-18, Batla House on 19 September 2008 by firing at the police party. He was later arrested and put to trial in the encounter case. He has been convicted by the trial court in 2013.

Sharfuddin (Azamgarh module) along with Atif Ameen went to Pakistan for training in 2004.

Syed Abdul Karim, alias Tunda (LeT), was involved in the 1993 serial train blasts that shook Mumbai. He fled to Bangladesh/ Pakistan after the CBI cracked these cases. There, he joined the LeT. He established resident agents in India. They caused 42 blasts in and around Delhi in 1996–97. In 1998, the group was caught by the Crime Branch of the Delhi Police. He was later arrested by the Special Cell of the Delhi Police in August 2013 from the Indo-Nepal border.

Yasin Bhatkal (Pune module) took training in Pakistan in the end of 2005. He is an expert in bomb-making. He prepared bombs for the court blasts in UP and also for the Hyderabad, Jaipur, Gujarat and Delhi blasts. After the Batla House encounter, he became the head of IM in India and caused many blasts till his arrest in 2011.

Zia-ur-Rehman (Azamgarh module) was involved in the Ahmedabad and Delhi blasts of 2008.

Zeeshan Ahmad, alias Amir Talha (Azamgarh module), took part in the Ahmedabad and Delhi blasts of September 2008.

ACKNOWLEDGEMENTS

This world is a safer place because of people who are fighting terrorism on the front line. Without my experiences at the Special Cell of leading a team of extremely hard-working, talented and committed policemen, this book would not have been possible.

Thank you to all the women and men at the Special Cell, whose work and dedication inspire excellence. A special shout-out to Alok Kumar, Sanjeev Kumar Yadav, Ravi Shankar, Dharmender Kumar, Ravinder Kumar Tyagi, Rahul Kumar Singh, Sanjay Dutt and Rajan Bhagat, for helping me revisit the memories associated with this case, which has helped me put this book together.

A very special thanks to my seniors, Shri Tejinder Khanna and Shri Yudhvir Singh (Y.S.) Dadwal, who believed in our team and supported us through several ups and downs during this journey.

I am eternally grateful to all the exemplary leaders from the IB and the Delhi Police for their constant guidance during my time at the Special Cell. Their good counsel and unwavering support shaped my counterterror investigative skills which, in turn, guided me and my team in cracking tough cases.

To my parents, Omperkash and Shanti Devi. I am forever indebted to you for imparting valuable lessons that have given me the strength to fight through adversity and to have faith in the power of karma.

Words cannot express the gratitude I feel towards my family for their support during this journey. My wife, Renuka—your love and kindness have been the cornerstone of my life. My daughter, Shruti—my deepest appreciation for the hours you have invested in helping me at every step of this book, in reading the drafts and sharing your insights. A heartfelt thank you to Kritika, Archit and Sharad for always being my pillars of strength and encouragement.

A big thank you to the Rupa team for its editorial support, which helped me transform my experiences into a book.

To the citizens of my country—I heartily thank you for being a source of strength and motivation while discharging our duties.